DRUGS & YOUTH

Marijuana plants, 10–12 feet high

DRUGS & YOUTH

Medical
Psychiatric
and Legal
Facts

Joseph H. Brenner, M.D.

Medical Department, Massachusetts Institute of Technology
Director, Cambridgeport Medical Clinic, Cambridge, Massachusetts

Robert Coles, M.D.

University Health Services, Harvard University

Dermot Meagher

Former Assistant District Attorney, Worcester, Massachusetts
Fellow, Harvard Center for Criminal Justice, 1970–71

 LIVERIGHT | New York

The chapter "Flying high or low" was originally published as "Drugs,
Flying High and Flying Low" in *The Yale Review*. Copyright © 1967 by
Yale University. Reprinted by permission of the publisher.

1.987654321

Standard Book Number: cloth   87140-501-6
                       paper 87140-028-6
Library of Congress Catalog Card Number: 72–114383

Designed by Charlotte Thorp

Manufactured in the United States of America

We dedicate this book to America's children—who one day, we can only hope, will not grow up to bear arms abroad or at home bear witness to officially sanctioned greed, bitterness, and meanness—all clothed in the grandest, most pious of words.

| Contents

| Preface

Millions of parents, millions of young people all over the country are trying to make sense of the "drug scene." How many people are part of that scene? How do they fare, both in the short run and over a longer span of time? Some who question are curious observers; some are themselves "into drugs" and want to know all there is to know. And, of course, there are the many who don't care to question, who have already decided what they think and feel, want done or want to do—positions which unfortunately are not always based on accurate information and rational discussion.

We want to make something very clear at the outset; we are not writing this book to pile up before the reader's eyes our share of unequivocal and insistently authoritative claims. We are two doctors and a lawyer; each of us has had rather a lot to do with the various medical, psychiatric, and legal problems that accompany the use of drugs. But, like most everyone who struggles with this problem today—parents and children, teachers and principals, the police and the courts, legislators in city halls, state capitals, and the Congress—we must struggle on our own, because the answers to utterly important questions, to controversial allegations, are not yet established.

By definition the clinician tries to see each person as an individual, and the lawyer similarly takes on a particular client, one who may be involved in a difficulty that many others have faced, but who, nevertheless, presents to the law a unique life with its own particular assets and liabilities. But doctors and lawyers live and work in a particular society at a particular moment in that society's history. When social changes begin to take place, when customs and attitudes undergo slow but noticeable modification, doctors and lawyers are often among the first to meet up with the results—the confusion and worry individuals feel, the troubles they encounter with the law. They may also be among the first, ironically, to sense that something much more far-reaching is happening; not simply has an individual gone astray, but a whole series of beliefs, a whole way of life, is under scrutiny if not assault. One can insist upon one's obligation to work with the individual, yet inadvertently come face to face with larger issues, broader problems, controversies that are social, cultural, and historical in nature.

As doctors and lawyers, we have watched a patient, client, or accused person become much more—something W. H. Auden has called "a whole climate of opinion." No longer can even the most determined clinician or lawyer ignore the present climate, not when thousands and thousands of youths in schools and colleges take a drug like marijuana, admit to doing so, and present a rather casual account of the experience to the observer—be he friendly, relatively indifferent, or thoroughly critical. The issue is not one of mere numbers; what is taking place has to do with a feeling shared by a growing minority that something like marijuana is to be tried, if not used, almost as a matter of course, that is, with a certain conventionality. It is always hard to know precisely when such a feeling becomes established, when the isolated acts of a few, or the prevalent acts of very distinct and special groups, become more pervasively the interest and concern of a nation's youth. Statistics and responses to polls and questionnaires tell something; but the social historian, the teacher, the doctor, lawyer, or minister, not to mention the observant (and troubled) parent or young person, can quite often make his own decision on the basis of what he sees, hears and experiences. Any intelligent person can decide for himself, for example, that the use of marijuana is illegal, shunned by many, criticized on thoroughly believable and justifiable grounds by many more, but is nevertheless enough of a commonplace thing to warrant the conclusion that a once relatively rare and forbidden kind of behavior has become not only fashionable but a well known, familiar, and established practice, if still a legally prohibited one, for many.

We do not want to dwell primarily on this "climate of opinion," but like millions of other Americans we would be fools if we didn't think about such things, particularly in view of the work we do in clinics and courthouses—much of it among young people. We want to set forth here as clearly as we can whatever medical, psychiatric and legal information we have come by as men ourselves troubled and confused by what is happening among us with drugs. The questions most readers ask are also our questions: What is one to make of the rising involvement of a rich nation's middle-class youth with a drug like marijuana—and with other drugs? What exactly is heroin or LSD or marijuana, what does it do to the body, to the mind, to a person's spirit, his values, his idea of what matters and what is utterly unimportant? And the laws that tell us which drugs are allowed and which are forbidden, how are we to make sense of them, come to terms with them, live under them—today and in the coming years when the disparity between what is legally sanctioned and what is commonly done may grow wider?

We also want to state explicitly that we are not writing this book to "defend" the use of marijuana—or any other drug—or to "attack" that same use. We have talked at length about the drug scene with one another (and with many colleagues, friends, patients, and clients). We have had a fair share of involvement in that scene. One of us has had to prosecute dozens and dozens of so-called marijuana cases—cases that involved, in legal terms, possession of the drug, selling it, being found in its presence—as well as cases having to do with other drugs. One of us has practiced medicine all over the world and has seen a wide variety of drugs used for an equally wide variety of social, philosophical, and religious as well as medical purposes; now, while practicing both medicine and psychiatry in an American university setting and directing a medical clinic whose specific aim has been to bring physicians into useful contact with young people, he has worked with many youths who use drugs, call themselves "alienated," or better, feel so without using such words. One of us, as a child psychiatrist, has studied a number of social and political struggles in an effort to find out how youths become involved in social action, why some youths, instead of or along with this involvement, turn to drugs; studied how ghetto children grow up in contrast to middle-class children, with the matter of drugs and their meaning no insignificant question in this research.

We hope that our work, our interests, and involvements will not be viewed as yet another mass of credentials designed to shower a rightfully inquiring public with rhetoric and to lead that public toward a neat, clear-cut "position." We frankly don't have one and want to say so here and now. We have some ideas, some feelings, some things we want to suggest, uphold, take issue with, strongly condemn; but we will tend to zig-zag, argue with ourselves, talk pro and con, and most of all, we hope, avoid certain polemic postures that by now have become a familiar part of such criticisms: moralistic condemnation; ecstatic approval of an almost messianic kind; naive skirting of the issue; and finally, the resort to illogical or unproved generalizations that can be used to attack or defend almost anything, especially something as controversial as drugs.

In the pages that follow we will become more specific about the ways in which men deal with issues that are intricate, unsettling, puzzling, and charged with all sorts of medical, psychiatric, and legal contradictions. We hope our attempt will cause at least a few readers to think about the various problems, clarify a few things for some who have not completely made up their minds, as well as help clarify some things for ourselves; because like thousands of youths and their parents we are constantly being asked to decide, take a stand, make clear how we feel, what we have to say, suggest, and recommend.

What we have done, we have done together. We have

divided up the task of writing in accordance with our training and experience. We have viewed the subject from three perspectives—the medical, the psychiatric, and the legal. But a book written today on drugs and youth cannot escape touching on the social, cultural, and political forces that hover over and stick fast to such a subject, cannot avoid looking at these forces, and, perhaps, being taken for one of them itself.

DRUGS & YOUTH

| Definitions

There has been no shortage of enthusiastic spokesmen who have tried to label different drugs with the emotionally laden term *narcotic*—a word associated with abuse, addiction, destruction of mind and body, crimes of violence, and heavily restrictive and punitive legal codes. Narcotics, in the strict medical sense, are a very small group of drugs: opium and its active constituents, most common of which are morphine and codeine, and heroin, a derivative of morphine that was synthesized (made chemically in the laboratory) late in the nineteenth century. To this group several drugs with opiumlike properties that have been synthesized more recently can legitimately be added; such as demerol, which is the brand name given to meperidine hydrochloride, and methadone, although prolonged use of this drug is much less destructive to mind and body than morphine or heroin.

Narcotics have the common properties of inducing sleep or stupor, frequently accompanied by euphoria, and pleasant dreams or fantasies; and, of course, they can give enormous relief from physical and mental pain. Unfortunately, narcotics are seriously addictive, and the body rapidly develops a tolerance to their use. (The terms *addiction* and *tolerance* will be defined later in this chapter.)

Narcotics can be abused, severely so, by people whose pain comes not from physical illness, but is surely as real and unpleasant—we refer to those brutalized by and trapped in the ghettoes of our cities. In those ghettoes great numbers of people, mostly black, suffer, and suffer, and suffer. Existing social and medical services have not been able to cope with the rage and the pain of the human beings trapped there. Narcotics offer one route of escape, an awful and ravaging route—a pathway of despair followed when personal and social pain becomes unbearable, and relief otherwise unobtainable. Testifying at a recent Black Panther trial in New York City, a witness told of becoming addicted to heroin at the age of thirteen: "[Heroin helped] my nose not to smell the urine-soaked hallways. I didn't feel the garbage underfoot. I didn't hear the sound of police sirens tearing through the black jungle."

Before the Harrison Narcotic Act of 1914 there were no effective controls over the use of narcotics in the United States. Indeed, through the nineteenth century and up until 1914, narcotics had been used in great quantities, and a large number of patent medicines were freely advertised and could be bought openly and cheaply. It has been estimated that, before narcotics were brought under federal control by the Harrison Act, one in four hundred of the population of the United States was addicted to opium or its derivatives. Among those addicted there was probably a preponderance of white women who were poor and had no easy access to physicians. The simplest remedy to ease physical pain was to buy a cheap narcotic preparation, and frequent use often led to addiction. At that time there was no black market in narcotics and no known correlation between their use and the crimes of the urban poor. After the Harrison Act went into effect, the rate of addiction is said to have fallen to one in four thousand. These figures cannot be assumed accurate, or even nearly accurate, because of the enormous difficulties in getting such information, but unquestionably the Harrison Act greatly reduced the number of people addicted to narcotics in the United States.

What became of those people addicted to narcotics? In the years immediately following the passage of the Harrison Act, medical help was relatively easy to get, and most addicts managed to conquer their addiction. In 1919 the first of a number of ambulatory drug clinics opened in New York City. These clinics had as their goals the rehabilitation of the addict and, hopefully, to protect thousands of citizens from the criminal elements which were beginning to dominate the drug scene even then.

Shortly after 1919 federal treasury officials, whose task it was to police the Harrison Act, began campaigning for an increasingly punitive policy towards addicts as well as sellers and pushers of drugs. The press took up the cry, and public outrage against the addict markedly increased. By 1923 all the clinics had closed. The addicts, now labeled as criminals or moral degenerates, were no longer viewed as human beings in terrible distress and in need of medical care. Once seen as unwitting victims of drug abuse, they had now become enemies of the people. (The Harrison Act made no attempt to interfere with the right of physicians to prescribe opiates and synthetic narcotics for legitimate medical purposes. The drugs continue to be widely and appropriately used for the control of severe pain, diarrhea, and cough. Physicians recognize the dangers

5

inherent in the uncontrolled use of narcotics and are in agreement that controls are necessary.)

Marijuana, however, when viewed with even minimal scientific objectivity, cannot be called a narcotic, for it has totally different pharmacological properties and clinical effects than the group of drugs described above. How then did it come to be classified as a narcotic?

Until the late 1920s marijuana was in common use in only the southern and southwestern regions of the United States, and most marijuana users were Mexican-Americans. But gradually during the 1920s and 1930s marijuana use began spreading among the poor, predominantly in rural areas where the hemp plant, which is the source of marijuana, was readily available. Hemp had been planted as a commercial crop in many parts of the nation for many years, for the plant grows very easily in hot, dry climates. In the days before the invention and development of newer, stronger synthetic fibers, such as nylon and dacron, the tough fiber of the stems of the tall male hemp (cannabis) plant was in great demand for the manufacture of rope and other materials, which made hemp a valuable cash crop.

But the hemp plant yielded something in addition to fiber for making ropes. Smoking the crushed leaves of the female plant, and to a lesser extent those of the male plant, produced in the user a pleasant sense of euphoria and relaxation, often enough without a hangover or other unpleasant side effects. Moreover, smoking marijuana was cheaper than smoking tobacco; in fact, it was absolutely free to most of its users. Also, marijuana was used by many for its calming and tranquilizing effects, no small thing for fearful men and women.

Eventually the use of marijuana spread from the rural areas to the cities, but again, predominantly among the poor.

6

At the same time smaller special groups, among them artists and jazz musicians, were smoking marijuana, not only for the relaxation and euphoria that it produced but also for particular effects on their aesthetic sensibilities, or so they claimed.

One can only speculate on the reasons for the massive attack on marijuana, spearheaded by the Federal Bureau of Narcotics and supported by Congress, that took place in the 1930s. At the time that this attack was mounting, marijuana was not smoked by students or middle- and upper-class whites, but in the main by poor blacks and poor whites whose roots were in rural America. The depression, which brought mass migration from the country to the cities, accounted partly for the upsurge in marijuana use in the cities, along with a number of other social and political changes. The country was beaten down; with the collapse of the economy came massive unemployment, hunger, malnutrition, and despair. An anxious, nervous Congress was told that marijuana was eating its way into the very soul of the nation, ravaging bodies and minds—a clear and present danger to society. And if the depression was not so easy to abolish, the use of marijuana certainly could be forbidden. The campaign to outlaw marijuana was led by the Federal Bureau of Narcotics, a government agency created in 1930. Appointed to head the new bureau was Harry J. Anslinger, who held the position from 1930 until 1962. (Mr. Anslinger has since become the United States delegate to the United Nations Commission on Narcotics.)

The Federal Bureau of Narcotics subjected the press and Congress to a steady stream of alarming statements concerning marijuana—statements that were frightening, lurid, and sometimes tantalizing. Again and again the accusations were made: that marijuana drove people to violence, crime, sexual excess, and even madness; that it sapped the will, destroyed

7

the moral fiber, and frequently led the user to opium and heroin addiction. Marijuana was a terrible curse visited on the nation and had to be eradicated.

In 1937 the Marijuana Tax Act was passed, attaching severe penalties to the possession of even the smallest amount of the herb. In 1961 Mr. Anslinger reflected:

As the marihuana situation grew worse, a new action had to be taken to get proper control legislation passed. By 1937, under my direction, the Bureau launched two important steps: one, a legislative plan to seek from Congress a new law that would place marihuana and its distribution directly under federal control; secondly, on radio and on major forums, such as that presented annually by the New York *Herald Tribune,* I told the story of this evil weed of the fields and riverbeds and roadsides. I wrote articles for magazines; our agents gave hundreds of lectures to parents, educators, social and civic leaders. In network broadcasts I reported on the growing list of crimes, including murder and rape. I described the nature of marihuana and its close kinship to hashish. I continued to hammer at the facts. I believe we did a thorough job, for the public was alerted, and the laws to protect them were passed, both nationally and at the state level.

The Federal Bureau of Narcotics actually resorted to an old Arabic fable for supporting evidence that use of hashish, the concentrated resin from the hemp plant, could put a man in the frame of mind for committing murder. Long ago, toward the end of the eleventh century, there is said to have lived a man named Hassan who was determined that his name would never die, that even if his sons' sons begat no sons, his name would be made to live on as long as men have a language to speak. Hassan was a resourceful person who, like Marco Polo, had travelled through Asia, learning many things. From India he brought the hemp plant to introduce to his Middle Eastern

8

countrymen, who delighted in the sticky, resinous substance that the plant exudes. So, the fable has it, the substance was called hashish after the traveller's name, Hassan. Like many men of imagination, Hassan did not rest his talents there, but also expounded the virtues of political murder as opposed to murder for reasons of personal hatred. Once more the name of Hassan was immortalized, this time in the word *assassin*.

The story of Hassan, like most fables, has many variations, but the association of the words *hashish* and *assassin* is indeed misleading. Apart from the tales of the redoubtable Hassan, there is no reliable evidence in the long-recorded history of marijuana and hashish to suggest that their use leads to violence. Nevertheless, a systematic and relentless campaign against marijuana in the 1930s raged so successfully that by the time hearings were held before the House Committee on Ways and Means, opposition was slight. The chief witness in both the House and the Senate hearings was Mr. Anslinger, who repeatedly recited frightening tales of crimes committed by persons under the influence of marijuana. In 1937 the Marijuana Tax Act was passed and from that time on, by federal law, marijuana has in effect been treated as a narcotic drug, although with one major difference. Since it is not considered to have medicinal values not already available in medicines and since its other unique effects are not considered medicinal, marijuana has been barred even from prescription by physicians.

In any event, federal law or no law, words like *habituation, dependence, tolerance,* and *addiction* have always been used rather freely. Because the same word can have very different meanings in the minds of different people, thus causing a great deal of confusion, reasonable working definitions of these

9

terms follow. They are not dictionary definitions, which are too brief to be adequate and cannot meet the complexities of this highly charged area of human concern.

Habituation

Of all the terms that are used to describe the state or dilemma of the user of drugs, *habituation* is, or should be, the least troublesome. Ordinarily when we speak of habits we indifferently label them good or bad; we see them more or less as personal qualities or characteristics of individuals. However, when the word *habit* or *habituation* is applied to drugs, a dismaying emotionalism and vagueness creep in. The fact is that all of us are creatures of habit. Our daily lives are largely filled with repetitive functions, some of which, like eating, sleeping, and excreting, are necessary for the ordinary business of caring for the body's needs. There are other habits that we are trained to adopt in order to go about the business of living: for example, we have our automobile motors regularly tuned up, and we take care of our monthly accounts. Thus habits are both public and private in nature, and without them, without a certain repetitiveness, our lives would tend to become chaotic. Habituation helps us give order to our lives. Some habits relate to our public lives: we are students, bus drivers, doctors, or policemen. Society sanctions most occupations, which again involve daily habits and routines. Other habits are not strictly essential to the functioning of society. They are personal, private, and idiosyncratic, and they often apply to a particular person's idea of pleasure.

Thus, a man and his wife come together at the end of a

working day, and they touch, kiss, and caress. Have they not done these same things a thousand times before, and will they not continue to do them in the future? How pleasant, how satisfying, to be habituated to the kiss, the touch, the gentle word. The same couple has its habits of eating, of drinking, of smoking, of musical taste, and of recreation. When looking at ourselves honestly, we can usually separate those of our habits that we believe good and those that we believe bad, although the separation is, beyond a certain point, arbitrary and personal. But generally we suppose that good habits are those that add a pleasurable, or at least satisfying, dimension to our lives or the lives of others, and that bad habits are those that diminish us or our fellow men. Yet, when the habit is essentially private, who is to judge whether it is good or bad?

Many people enjoy a glass of wine at dinner or a nightcap of brandy. The repetitive act of taking a favorite drink every day is indeed a habit. It could be called an indulgent habit, and those who believe that drinking alcohol of any kind in any amount is immoral would call it a bad habit. But for the habituated—those who delight in the sensuous aroma, the golden liquid, the pungent taste, the suffusion of warmth— the experience is most pleasurable. It is, to them, a good habit. When there is no dependence or craving, it is a simple habit, one not willingly given up. If there is no dependence or no addiction to alcohol, one can be deprived of it without physical suffering or mental collapse—although, if one is habituated to something, to do without that thing could indeed be felt as deprivation. On the other hand, many millions of persons in the United States take different drugs habitually, by prescription and nonprescription; and a good number of those come to be dependent on them, a word that we come to next.

11

Dependence

Dependence need not be an imprecise or ambiguous term, for its meaning, when applied to drugs, is only slightly different from its regular usage. What differentiates *dependence* from *habit*? When a person "depends" on something or someone, it is implied that without that support he would suffer a state of disequilibrium. He might or might not be able to take steps to restore his equilibrium by shifting dependence to another direction or by readjusting his needs.

For example, a widow may be largely dependent on a son for financial and emotional support. If he suddenly dies, she has no choice but to make adaptations in her life by changing her pattern of living. She may succeed; she may compensate for the abrupt removal of material and psychological supports. But if not, she will continue to feel deprivation, emotional as well as physical, even after she has stopped mourning her son.

Turning back to drugs, a distinction is often drawn between physical dependence and psychological dependence. To some extent this is an arbitrary separation, because there are usually both physical and psychological aspects to a person's dependence. However, one or the other usually predominates. Two examples: 1. A person with severe chronic arthritis may be dependent on one drug for pain, on another drug to relieve inflammation, and yet on another to help him sleep. There may be only a tiny psychological component to his several drug dependencies, and so they could clearly be called physical. 2. Another person, with no physical disorder, takes the same dose of Nembutal or Seconal (trade names for barbiturate compounds) night after night for many years to induce sleep, without having to increase the dose and without deleterious effects. This kind of dependence is preponderantly psychological.

A great deal of publicity has recently focused, and justifiably so, on the excessive and sometimes promiscuous use of legally prescribed stimulants and sedatives. It is true that many millions of Americans have become psychologically dependent on drugs to help them sleep. Yet, despite all the abuses, for a portion of these millions (how large is unknown) the regular use of sleeping pills is a necessary blessing. It is not unreasonable to ask, however, if something other than drugs could take the place of the sleeping pill. One can say that there must be some cause or causes for chronic insomnia and that those causes should be identified and then cured. But often there is a great gulf between diagnosis and cure. Where are the doctors and the psychiatrists with the time to listen and listen and advise and advise? Where is the money to pay them? For many people, to whom life's minor hurts and pains seem ever-present and impossible of solution, a symptomatic remedy such as a pill before retiring seems terribly important. And for a busy physician the sleeping pill prescription is a handy solution when he is asked for help. Some doctors would therefore argue that the psychological dependence of the insomniac can be just as legitimate as the physical dependence of the arthritic.

Psychological dependence on drugs can also be a problem for the young for very particular reasons. Adolescence is a tumultuous time—a fact that adults too frequently fail to appreciate. (Human beings have a remarkable, perhaps fortunate, capacity for blocking out painful events and periods in their lives. Readers who doubt this might reflect on their own adolescence to see how much or little they can remember.) The adolescent must cope with many difficult psychological tasks,

13

including the need to decrease his dependence on protective parents and thereby achieve separateness. He must struggle to arrive at some sense of who he is and where he stands in relation to the rest of the world. This struggle is never without anguish; it brings recurring uncertainty, self-doubt, and sometimes out-right despair. Some adolescents find the idea of escape through the use of drugs, such as marijuana, attractive, and the idea sometimes includes the illusion that mastery lies in self-knowl-edge through drugs.

It is, therefore, not too difficult to understand why the young might be particularly vulnerable to the seductive prom-ises of marijuana and other "mind-expanding" drugs. If psy-chological dependence *does* develop, the capacity to make the difficult adolescent adjustments may be impaired.

But with marijuana, psychological dependence is gen-erally not a problem. Of the great number of adolescents and young adults who smoke marijuana, only a very small per-centage become psychologically dependent on it. Admittedly, those few are indeed in trouble. The dependency, however, is determined much more by the particular drabness, pain, and ugliness of their lives and of the immediate world in which they live than by the actual smoking of marijuana, in what-ever quantity.

Tolerance

The term *tolerance* has a very specific meaning—the ability of the body to build up a degree of resistance or immunity to a drug, so that increasing amounts must be taken in order to achieve the same effects. Tolerance can be developed to some drugs but not to others, and, to be brief and blunt, why this

14

is so is a mystery. A drug with a most alarming ability to build up bodily tolerance is methamphetamine, commonly known as speed. When this drug is prescribed, as it frequently is, to control excessive weight, the recommended dose is usually five milligrams to be taken three times daily. However, many young people take speed illegally for the effects described in a later chapter. These people find that their bodies can build up such a huge tolerance to the drug that within a very few weeks they may need to inject as much as five thousand milligrams directly into the bloodstream (a practice called "shooting speed" or "mainlining," although the latter term is usually reserved for heroin) to achieve the desired effects. Like speed, the narcotic group of drugs described earlier gives rise to varying degrees of tolerance. But there are many drugs that do not cause tolerance; one of them is marijuana.

Addiction

Addiction to a drug takes place when profound changes occur in the chemistry and physiology, or the workings, of the body —profound, but reversible, changes. Only certain drugs cause addiction. Drug addiction is a phenomenon that is not completely understood. It is as if the natural chemicals of the body move over to accommodate the interloper, the addictive drug, so that near normal bodily functions can go on only when a continual supply of the drug is pumped into the system. When one thinks of addiction, inevitably heroin springs to mind. Heroin is indeed the most addictive of drugs, although all of the true narcotics are addictive to a lesser degree. The person who is addicted suffers painful withdrawal symptoms if the supply of the addictive drug is stopped abruptly. For example,

15

a chronic alcoholic upon withdrawal may "go into the DTs" (*delirium tremens*) with convulsions, hallucinations, and feelings of terror; the person addicted to barbiturates (used ordinarily for sedation or sleep) will suffer severe irritability and insomnia, possibly accompanied by convulsions seven to ten days after withdrawal. Fortunately, the withdrawal symptoms can be greatly modified and danger diminished with good medical care. It is clear that the chemical system of the body takes an appreciable time to adjust to functioning without the addictive drug.

Alcohol is an addictive agent, not only to the chronic alcoholic whom America possesses in such great number but also to the millions more who know that they must take two or more drinks in the middle of a working day in order to, as they often put it, "feel halfway normal." Some of them may deny it, but these people are addicted. If they could not take the alcohol, they would feel physically unwell and their functions would be impaired.

| Marijuana

Marijuana, obtainable widely but illegally in the United States, is a finely ground, dried herb that looks somewhat like a cross between shredded green tobacco and oregano. It has only a faint smell when dried, but when smoked gives off a characteristic pungent, aromatic odor that is easily recognizable to anyone who has smelled it before. The active chemical ingredients—that is to say, the ingredients that cause the psychological changes so enormously controversial—are contained in a resin within the leaves and topmost flowers of the female Indian hemp plant, *cannabis indica* (or *cannabis sativa*). The male plant contains a similar, perhaps identical, substance, but in much smaller amounts. Given favorable conditions for growth, the resin will actually ooze from the surface of the leaves of the female plant and can easily be separated in a variety of ways. The resin from the topmost leaves and flowers is the most potent of the preparations.

In many parts of the world, particularly in India, the

17

Middle East, and North Africa, the use of cannabis has been sanctioned for many centuries, and various names are used for different preparations of the plant. In India *charras* is the name of the concentrated resin—prepared as flattened, rounded, or oval cakes, brown in color, or as a paler, more granular substance—extracted from the flowers or fruit that grow at the tops of the female plant. The paler substance, believed by some to have more subtle effects, can be produced also by treating the brown resin with steam. *Charras* is the equivalent of the Middle East's *hashish. Ganja* is a less potent resin obtained from the lower leaves of the plant, and *bhang,* or *dagga,* resembles most closely the marijuana of the Western Hemisphere; however, these preparations are much more commonly swallowed than smoked. In most of the states of India the use of *bhang* is legal and subject to minimal but apparently effective controls. Many thousands of small stores have licenses, renewable each year, to sell *bhang,* and an attempt is made to restrict sales to persons eighteen and older. Because it has an unpleasant, bitter taste, *bhang* is commonly combined with more palatable ingredients, such as ice cream, or blended with spices and nuts in milk. Throughout most of India one need not walk very far for a drink of *bhang,* and its use is not considered to have created serious legal, public health, or moral problems. The crushed leaves of the marijuana plant have been a favorite ingredient in many recipes in Indian cooking, and in the halcyon days of the British raj, ladies from England commonly served afternoon tea cake prepared with marijuana.

Mexico has been the chief source of supply of marijuana to the United States. The drug is usually smuggled over the border in compressed blocks or bricks weighing one kilogram, which is a little over two pounds. Pushers or users then break

18

up the marijuana into amounts of approximately one-half ounce to one ounce, which are usually sold in small plastic sandwich bags. One of the many possible negative consequences of the recent massive attempt by United States customs officials to stop the flow of marijuana from Mexico is that traders in Mexico may prefer to deal in hashish rather than marijuana, because the great reduction in bulk would make smuggling easier. If this indeed happens, the campaign will have backfired, for hashish is much more potent than marijuana.

Although many different names are given to marijuana and hashish in this country, they do not indicate different potencies. In fact, all of the terms used to describe the products of the cannabis plant refer either to marijuana, the chopped and dried plant, or hashish, the different preparations of the resin. Some of the common names for marijuana are maryjane, pot, grass, boo, hay, tea, and weed. New situations breed new names, and the marijuana smoked by United States servicemen in Vietnam is sometimes called "Laotian green." Marijuana cigarettes are referred to as joints, sticks, or reefers, and the stub ends are called butts or roaches.

The history of marijuana

The earliest reference to cannabis appears in a work of pharmacy written by the Chinese emperor Shen-Neng in 2734 B.C., possibly two thousand years before the plant reached India. But it is in India that marijuana has been most carefully cultivated, highly valued, and widely used. Perhaps that is why marijuana was given the botanical name *cannabis indica,* or cannabis of India, rather than cannabis of China.

19

Indian literature is replete with references to the hemp plant, the different uses of which have been tightly interwoven with the fabric of Indian life. For at least two thousand years the drug has been richly used for medicinal, religious, social, and recreational purposes. Marijuana and hashish have been seen as protectors from evil influence, support in times of famine, stimulants to labor, a source of self-confidence, the key to divine revelation, and, by Indians of the nineteenth century, as the "poor man's heaven," "soother of grief," and "heavenly guide." Indeed, the wide use of marijuana is not surprising in India—a highly civilized country with a complex culture, diverse religions, and exquisite art forms, where appreciation of the aesthetic and fine regard for individual feelings are by tradition highly valued; a country where sensuousness has not withered before waves of self-hate; and a country devoted to inwardness and contemplation. Once the peculiar qualities of its resin were recognized, the hemp plant came to be cultivated and tended with great care. It was learned that the quality of the resin, as measured by its effects, was not dependent solely on the vagaries of climatic conditions—such as heat and drought—but also on techniques of horticulture.

From India the use of marijuana spread to the Middle East and other countries bordering on the eastern Mediterranean, including Greece. In the fifth century B.C. Herodotus recorded that the citizens of Scythia and Thrace made clothing from the hemp fibers and also "derived much merriment" from roasting the seeds of the plant and inhaling the intoxicating vapors. Many centuries passed before the use of marijuana spread to western Europe, where it was apparently introduced by Napoleon's army returning home from Egypt. It is not clear how and when cannabis came to the New World, but by the nineteenth century it was extensively used in Central America, South America, and Mexico. Not until around 1920, however, was it introduced in significant quantities in the United States.

Botany of marijuana

Cannabis sativa, the Indian hemp plant, grows in an extraordinary variety of climates and soils, including those of most parts of the United States, but it always requires heat for growth. The plant thrives in the hot, dry climate of Mexico and the southern United States, but it also grows rather well across the Great Plains, the Middle West, and the Northeast.

Cannabis sativa is a tall, stringy plant that grows literally like a weed—that is to say, with little or no care and attention. A mature plant varies in height from three to ten feet, depending on the quality of the seed and the growing conditions. Cannabis leaves are long and thin, dark green, and pointed at both ends, with notched or serrated edges.

Like most wild plants, the cannabis grown in one area is not identical with that grown in another, or even with that grown at a different time in the same place. Thus, there is marked variation in the quality and quantity of the active chemical substances contained in hashish and marijuana.

Cannabis can be improved and modified by careful horticulture, as it has been for many centuries in India and Asia. Users and dealers of the products of the cannabis plant in the Middle East and India speak, like wine connoisseurs, of vintage years—of good and not-so-good years—and the subtle variations are greatly appreciated by the cognoscenti.

21

Chemistry and pharmacology of cannabis

The complex chemistry of the substances contained in the cannabis resin is slowly being unraveled. Although well within the capability of a number of chemists in the United States, this task has been largely neglected until recently. Several factors underlie this neglect: the difficulty in obtaining supplies legitimately, the understandable fear and anxiety of scientists to carry out the required research, and the reluctance of sponsoring institutions to become involved in controversial issues. Such attitudes clearly reflect those of society at large, as a wealth of material attests. By way of example, here is a simple quotation from the first sentence of an editorial in the *Wall Street Journal* dated 25 March 1968: "We are not especially eager to discuss the unpleasant subject of marihuana." After this revealing opening, the editorial ironically goes on to plead for more research and more understanding in a less emotional climate.

So far, a number of marijuana's active chemicals have been isolated. Those of greatest interest form a group called the tetrahydrocannabinols, which appears to cause the drug's desired effects. It should be emphasized, however, that other chemicals present in the cannabis resin, while not in themselves psychoactive, might have a special combined, or synergistic, effect with the tetrahydrocannabinols.

Chemists have also discovered that the balance of different chemicals in the resin varies greatly with the growing conditions of the plant. For example, in the northeastern United States (where the growing season is short and the climate moderate), the marijuana is less potent than that grown in a warmer climate, because the resin contains a greater prepon-

22

derance of chemicals that cause no apparent psychological changes in the user.

At the same time that the chemical components of marijuana are being subjected to systematic quantitative and qualitative analysis, scientists are beginning to learn how to synthesize (manufacture in a laboratory) some of its chemicals. In 1965 two chemists, Mechoulam and Paoni, reported in the *Journal of the American Chemical Society* the first synthesis of a pure cannabis substance—delta-trans-tetrahydrocannabinol—which is probably the most psychoactive of the chemicals in the cannabis resin.

This synthetic substance, known as THC, has been circulating illegally in many of our cities since approximately 1967. But as with many other substances in the illicit drug world, where controls and standardization are virtually absent, what is represented as THC actually could be an extract of the cannabis plant or the uncertain products of crude syntheses—and hence the danger to all would-be users. Do they ever know what they are really getting?

The pharmacology and psychopharmacology of cannabis take us beyond the chemistry of the resin to a study of the observable effects on the body and mind of the human subject. How is the drug taken? What happens to the constituent chemicals in the body? What is the body's response to the drug? Is the drug toxic and, if so, on a short-term or long-term basis? How does the body rid itself of the drug?

Unfortunately, we cannot answer all these questions as fully as we should wish. The science of psychopharmacology is in its infancy. There is scarcely any information about how the majority of drugs affect the body and mind in the ways they do. For example, we do not even know how acetylsalicylic acid—more commonly known by its trade name, aspirin—

works. But this lack of knowledge does not prevent us from taking aspirin to ease simple headaches, to help bring down fever, or to lessen aches and pains, because we have learned from practical experience that aspirin can accomplish these purposes. An empirical, or experiential, approach governs much of the thought and method that underlies the development and use of a particular medicine for a particular purpose. By the same token, scrupulous attention must be given to unpleasant, unwanted, or dangerous side effects, and the purpose of many of our drug laws is to give us just such protection.

When we take note of the different ways in which the user may introduce the cannabis chemicals into his body, we immediately realize that some of the chemicals in hashish or marijuana may be filtered out or changed before entering the blood stream on their way to sites of action in the nervous system or elsewhere. Thus, to burn the resin or crushed leaves in a cigarette or pipe and inhale the smoke may introduce a different chemistry into the body than to roll crushed leaves into a tiny ball, flavor it with spices, and then swallow it.

Scientists have studied the chemical content of the marijuana smoke and the action of stomach secretions (which include very active enzymes and hydrochloric acid) on orally taken leaves. And so, some pharmacological data is known. Physiologically, the body's changes after using marijuana are not of enormous significance. There is often slight reddening of the conjunctiva, the membrane covering the whites of the eyes, so that the eyes may appear bloodshot. The size of the pupils is unaltered. Although it has commonly been stated that one sign of marijuana intoxication is enlargement of the pupils, this is not so. If the pupils are enlarged after using marijuana, it is probably because the lighting is dim. There is no change in the rate of respiration, but the heart rate is sometimes slightly, but apparently inconsequentially, increased. Blood pressure is unchanged. The mucous membrane, or lining, of the throat feels some irritation from inhalation of the smoke, but there is no evidence of chronic bronchitis or other lung disease as a consequence of repeated inhalation of marijuana smoke. The striking increase in appetite that occurs about thirty to sixty minutes after smoking marijuana is not related to any change in the blood sugar, and its cause and significance remain obscure.

It is believed that the body eliminates or destroys the cannabis chemicals within a few hours of ingestion without toxic residue. There are no lasting physical ill effects from the use of cannabis as far as anyone has been able to determine, and no death from its use has been reported. The psychological effects of marijuana are described later, but it can be said generally that, other factors being equal, the higher the dose the greater the effects, both physical and mental. As for our knowledge of exactly how the cannabis chemicals work on the body and mind, we are almost totally ignorant, and had better admit it.

One important observation is that most marijuana users learn very easily and quickly how to titrate, or measure, the dose when smoking. Experienced users take just enough to achieve the desired effects, and they usually want no more and take no more. This is true for hashish as well. Although hashish is much more potent than marijuana, there is no good evidence, either in this country or in the literature from other countries, to suggest that the experienced user of hashish has any more difficulty in controlling the amount of chemicals that he takes into his body than the user of marijuana. We are *not* saying that marijuana and hashish cannot lend themselves

25

to abuse, or overuse; we *are* saying that many users have learned quite successfully to take just enough and no more.

Experience of marijuana

Preliminary notes

Although an enormous amount of research remains to be done on the cannabis plant, its psychoactive products, and the long-term consequences of its use, a substantial body of information about marijuana already exists. The effects of marijuana on the human user can be described with some precision. To suggest otherwise would only increase the uncertainty and fears in the minds of legislators, lawyers, the police, and the public. In this regard a calm and rational approach is needed—an approach that allows existing evidence to be examined without passion or prejudgment, and further research to be undertaken in the quiet and efficient manner that characterizes other drug studies. Perhaps this is not possible because the use of marijuana has already become so controversial. Although the National Institute of Mental Health (a division of the United States Public Health Service) has expressed a willingness that is encouraging to spend more than one million dollars on marijuana research in 1970, even medical research is influenced by public attitudes. Both the design of an experiment and the ways the results are used mean as much as the number of dollars spent for the laboratory or clinical work.

Medical World News of September 1969 reported the following story of a physician, a clinical investigator in Texas. Earlier that year the physician was arrested by the state police for possession of marijuana, despite the fact that he had a federal

26

permit to grow marijuana for research use. He showed the arresting officer the permit, but nevertheless spent the night in the county jail before being released the next morning on a one thousand dollar bond. The physician maintained that he had suffered considerable harassment from both civil authorities and members of his own profession in the area. In the same issue of *Medical World News*, Dr. Andrew Weil of the National Institute of Mental Health, who with Zinberg and Nelsen wrote a research paper on marijuana for the December 1968 issue of the journal *Science,* is quoted:

The fact is that it is very difficult to do marihuana research, no matter what anyone tells you. The legal problems are still extraordinary, but I think the real problem is the emotional attitudes you run into in institutions. People are just scared of it, and they set obstacles in your path and force you to go through things that you just don't encounter in doing research of any other kind.

Effects of marijuana on the user

Before describing the complex effects of marijuana on the user, some general comments should be made about the considerable variability of the effects of the same drug (and this applies to virtually every entry in the pharmacopoeia) on *different* users and even on the *same* user at *different* times. And then, one must never forget that the quality or purity of the drug also varies. As long as marijuana remains an illegal drug, subject to only the crudest of quality controls, there can be no certainty as to what is contained in a particular reefer, or marijuana cigarette. The quantity and potency of the active substances vary enormously from batch to batch. To stretch it further, marijuana is often "cut"—mixed with other vegetable matter such as oregano—or for a complexity of reasons, it is often

27

adulterated with other substances which may themselves be extremely toxic or dangerous. This is done by unscrupulous, and often ignorant, distributors or pushers.

Basic to the various effects of marijuana is the *set*, or the mesh of variables in the mind and body of the user. An experiment with particular chemicals involving a human subject is different from an experiment with the same chemicals in a pure laboratory situation, without human participation. In a test tube all the variables—such as temperature, quantity, and presence of contaminants—can be controlled. But the human subject is of a different order of complexity than "another chemical." The total situation of the user at the time he takes a drug is referred to as the *set*. *Set*, then, is a complex of sorts, made up of the personality of the user, his mood, his expectations, and his immediate state of mind, including the presence or absence of fears or anxieties. Also included in the *set* is the user's physical state. Is he rested, or tired, or exhausted? The *set* also embraces the environment in which the drug is taken. Is the user alone or with others? Does he know his companions? Does he find them agreeable? Can he trust them? What is the physical setting? Is it comfortable, aesthetically pleasing, and quiet? Is there music to listen to, or is there a constant intrusion of strident street noises punctuated by ambulance and police sirens? The *set* even includes the larger social context in which the drug is taken. Thus, if the use of the drug is against the law with harsh penalties on the books, the user must be furtive for fear of a "bust," or arrest.

The importance of the *set* in determining the effects of marijuana cannot be overemphasized. For example, many users report that when they smoke in a situation where there is even the remotest possibility of detection and arrest, they note an increased tendency, while high, to experience sudden

28

periods of anxiety. In fact, they become anxiously convinced that they are about to be arrested and so experience fear and sometimes panic. Such episodes are usually fleeting, and reassurance from others present may serve to dispel quickly the fears as they arise. However, when these same users smoke the same material in other countries where the use of marijuana has clear social sanction and where the laws, if any, against its use are not commonly applied, they do not experience anything resembling that panic.

Many regular users of marijuana in this country smoke a reefer no more, and probably much less, than once or twice a week. There must be many who smoke perhaps half a dozen times a year. How does the use of marijuana affect them? Anyone who has smoked marijuana knows very well the importance of the *set* and soon learns, or should, not to smoke unless his mood, companions, and surroundings appear propitious for a pleasant experience. Many first-time marijuana smokers say that they feel no effects whatever, often because they have not learned the technique of smoking. The smoke must be inhaled deeply and held inside the lungs for a good period of time, say twenty seconds, before it is exhaled. Even when the smoke is properly inhaled, however, it is commonly reported that the first experience is not as pleasurable or intense as subsequent experiences. The explanation for this may well lie in psychological conditioning. If he knows what to expect, the user is better prepared for the experience. He is not apprehensive and is able to accept in a relaxed way the changes and feelings brought on by the drug—to enjoy the sensations without attempting to deny or fight them.

The following description of the effects of marijuana is approached from two standpoints: how the user *feels* and how he *behaves*. The *feelings* begin within about ten minutes after the smoke is first inhaled. An early sense of heaviness and warmth suffuses the muscular frame, especially around the shoulder girdle and the neck, although often the feeling spreads through the entire body. The heaviness is not unpleasant; it is really an awareness of one's body, of its tone, its presence. Ordinarily we are not aware of our bodies. In the Western world one of the definitions of good health is that all bodily functions are—to use a space age turn of phrase—"go" and automatic, so that we can concentrate on other matters.

The marijuana user becomes newly aware of his surroundings. He takes note of shapes, colors, and textures in a way that he has not done before. His perceptions and appreciations are not necessarily more profound, but he certainly sees things differently. His focus of interest shifts; atttention to objects waxes and wanes. The experience has an element of concreteness in that shapes, sounds, and colors are minutely examined. Listening to music becomes a total experience for the subject, who feels convinced that the structural components of the music are clearer, and therefore more beautiful, than ever before. Touch gives more pleasure and wonderment and seems more important, whether it be the touch of a fabric, a book, or another person. In addition, the "normal" separation between self and non-self seems less distinct and less necessary, for the user may no longer feel that he has a need to keep a safe distance between himself and other persons and objects in the outside world.

Generally, then, one can say that the use of marijuana can heighten perceptions and enhance appreciation. The subject may also relate a deep sense of "things falling into place," a new knowledge of "a harmonious order." Such assertions, of course, are intensely personal and subjective. The user's sense of time changes; after ten minutes he may think a whole hour has gone by. More commonly time is not measured; it just passes. Many users feel peaceful and relaxed, but they also experience an extraordinary lability, or changeability, of mood. A thought or remark might suddenly plunge the user into sadness, although he can just as rapidly recover, especially if a reassuring friend is present. A common experience, especially during the first one-half hour of intoxication, is a feeling of inner mirth that can readily advance to outward hilarity, with chuckling or laughing without any obvious external reason, as at a private joke. Essentially, however, the marijuana user's mood is one of quiet reflection with no great desire to go off and do things, of gentle warmth and passivity, and of benevolence and languor.

The following words by Baudelaire describe this experience beautifully and graphically:

It sometimes happens that your personality disappears, and you develop objectivity . . . to such an abnormal degree that the contemplation of outward objects makes you forget your own existence, and you soon melt into them. Your eye rests upon an harmoniously shaped tree bowing beneath the wind. Within a few seconds something that to a poet would merely be a very natural comparison becomes to you a reality. You begin by endowing the tree with your own passions, your desire or melancholy; its groanings and swayings become your own, and soon you *are* the tree. In the same way, a bird soaring beneath a blue sky, at first merely *represents* the immortal yearning to soar above human life; but already you are the bird itself.

The powers of concentration are, in one sense, impaired by marijuana ingestion. The user does not wish to stay with one line of thought for long and finds himself imperceptibly changing his focus of thought. If he really wants to concentrate on one issue, however, he can usually do so without difficulty.

If he knows that he has certain tasks that need to be done and believes in the value of these tasks, the marijuana user can accomplish them easily enough. Moreover, although he does not keep an eye on the clock (measured time having temporarily lost much of its meaning) he nevertheless is able to finish the tasks in no longer time than it takes otherwise. This is an important point, because a person high on marijuana usually does very little, and a frequent inference has been that such is the case because he is only able to do very little. A more accurate explanation is that a person about to smoke marijuana deliberately sets that time aside for reflection and relaxation.

Now we turn to the changes in *behavior* an individual demonstrates under the influence of marijuana. Speech is affected; the user's desire to talk decreases, and he is conscious that speech requires a certain physical effort, felt in the muscles around the mouth and throat. Indeed, psychologically he simply prefers not to speak. So, a person who has taken marijuana can seem silent. When he does speak, he appears ponderous and repeats himself, the repetition no doubt stemming from a desire to emphasize a seemingly worthwhile observation. The user will, however, often forget something he was about to say, because his thoughts and attention have drifted in another direction. He can engage in conversation and with a conscious effort he can converse with his usual intelligence, although the logical thread of a discussion may be lost if not guided by another person not under the influence of marijuana. But the user will usually convey by tone of voice and slowness of speech that he prefers infrequent use of words. He feels a desire to sense and appreciate things rather than talk about them. Rather than use his mind to communicate with others, he avoids use of his intellect and instead steeps himself in a satisfying richness of perception and feeling—or so he would describe it.

In regard to body movement, the person who has taken marijuana may wish to move around the room and enjoy a peculiarly pleasing sense of freedom of the body. He may dance to music, oblivious to others in the room unless they bring themselves to his attention; or he may want to move around as little as possible, to sit comfortably, or to lie down. He may experience a degree of lethargy, but no real desire to sleep; in fact, marijuana usually stimulates a desire to stay awake. The marijuana user rarely becomes aggressive or domineering; he commonly expresses a warm attitude of "live and let live" toward his fellow men. In contrast to a person intoxicated with alcohol, a person under the influence of marijuana exhibits little or no interest in driving a car. If anything, he becomes overly cautious, so that when he does get behind the wheel, he drives slowly and carefully. Although his coordination and space perception may be mildly impaired, they are usually in fact functioning better than he believes them to be—so his tendency is to overcompensate, to move slowly, deliberately, and safely. This strongly contrasts to the foolhardiness of the person under the influence of alcohol.

Marijuana has a variable effect on the physical as well as the emotional aspects of sexual intercourse, but the use of marijuana does not lead in itself to promiscuity or to sexual liaisons that may be later regretted. The actual effects of

33

marijuana on sexual desire, arousal, and performance are usually related quite directly to the sexual maturity and experiential knowledge of the user. Young persons who have not yet had sexual intercourse are not likely to be aroused by marijuana; in fact, if anything, many relate that in this respect grass turns them off. On the other hand, some who have enjoyed a steady sexual relationship with one partner have asserted that, after smoking marijuana and often for a day or two afterwards, the act of sexual intercourse becomes much more stimulating and satisfying. They claim to enjoy a fresh excitement and a new delight in their own and their partner's body.

Next we consider the less pleasant or toxic effects of marijuana and hashish. A difficulty arises immediately, for the word *toxic* means poisonous. Some of the unpleasant side effects of marijuana, such as nausea and vomiting, can clearly be called toxic, whereas other side effects are subjective, or "in the mind." So, we will refer inclusively to bad reactions, although their causes are probably toxic, whether at the level of finer brain functioning or at the more obvious level of bodily functioning.

Bad reactions to marijuana are related to one or more of three factors: the dose, the *set,* and the makeup of the user, chemical as well as psychological. With regard to *dose,* as long as the use of cannabis products remains illegal, the problems of contamination will exist. The contamination is sometimes accidental, or caused by ignorance, and sometimes deliberate. Many users will not try a new batch of marijuana without the assurance of a seller who can be trusted that he has tried it himself and that it passes muster. The concentration of psychoactive substances in the marijuana is important, for the drug's effects are often dose-related, but the user with even minimal experience is usually able to control the amount that he takes, as explained earlier.

The great complexity of variables called the *set* has been described in detail, and the *makeup* of the user, briefly referred to below, is covered more fully later. Oscar Wilde once wrote that the young men of London could be divided into two categories: the aesthetes and the hearties. The aesthetes presumably are more perceptive, more sensitive, and more emotional, and they understand the meaning of the raw-edged nerve. They are leaner and more pained by tragedy. The hearties, on the other hand, go through life cheerfully, either ignoring or not perceiving the world around them except as it pertains to their own well-being. The aesthetes, we suppose, might be attracted to marijuana and would be more likely to have strong psychological responses to it than the hearties, who would disdain it or, upon trying it, comment that it appeared to cause some throat irritation. Yet, how easy and how meaningless it is to make overly simple categorizations of human beings. Such categorizations often do violence to the complexity in all of us, to our "humanity"; and if the label or diagnosis that is attached to a person determines our thoughts and actions toward him, it can be downright dangerous.

In view of a well-recognized phenomenon—that the human response to many drugs is idiosyncratic—we can speak of a part of the makeup of the marijuana user as chemically grounded. It is not always possible to predict how a given dose of a pure drug will affect a particular person. When all other factors appear equal, we can only conclude that something in the chemical makeup of the body—possibly within the genes—determines that a greater or lesser amount of the drug is required in order to achieve the desired effect.

What are the bad reactions to marijuana?

1. *Nausea and vomiting* Nausea and vomiting are the most common acute toxic reactions to overdosage and do not appear to be serious. After the nausea subsides, the user usually feels well, sleeps soundly, and awakens in good spirits.

2. *Irritability and hypersensitivity to pain* Irritability and hypersensitivity to pain are variable reactions related most closely to the *set*. If he has been preoccupied with depressing problems or has felt harassed before smoking marijuana, or if, while high, his companions repeatedly press him to focus his attention on areas he would prefer to avoid, the user may experience waves of acute irritability. When other persons demonstrate support and reassurance to him, however, his irritability is usually short-lived. Often closely associated with irritability is hypersensitivity to pain. A minor physical hurt might develop into an acute pain accompanied by a strange sense of detachment. The pattern of provocation and relief is more or less the same as that of irritability described above.

3. *Suspiciousness, terror, and paranoia* Suspiciousness, terror, and paranoia are reactions primarily related to the *set,* especially to factors such as fear of detection and arrest. Personality factors are also important considerations. A subject who believes that affairs in his life never work out well or that he is not liked by others, has a tendency to experience brief spells of paranoia when under the influence of marijuana. He may irrationally accuse companions of harboring grudges against him or of deliberately setting out to hurt

him. If the physical surroundings are depressing—for example, if instead of music and a general atmosphere of relaxation, there are sounds of ugly quarreling from outside—the subject may become very upset. The drug seems to magnify the ugliness, and the user may feel trapped or really terrified. Such reactions, which are more likely after a drug overdose, are usually short-lived, although the subject may indeed need a great deal of patient, skillful reassurance.

4. *Changes in body image* Although changes in the body image are commonly pleasurable, some users experience what doctors call "a sense of loss of bodily boundaries" —a "fusion with the surroundings"—which carries with it, for many, a sense of impending "dissolution" that can lead to acute anxiety or panic. Unquestionably some users feel overwhelmed—lost, frightened, and alone. They are overcome with the strange sensation that their bodies will "melt away" and no longer be their own, but part of the world's property.

Before we turn to the problem of psychological dependence, let us observe what happens to the user who experiences a bad reaction and does not have an understanding companion to reassure and comfort him. Without this support his psychological distress, punctuated by short periods of pleasurable sensation, will last longer, but the total length of time for the effects of the marijuana to wear off usually will be unchanged. On rare occasions, he may undergo a fright reaction with paranoid feelings which possibly continue for a day or two, slowly diminishing.

5. *Psychological dependence and the pothead* Psychological dependence upon marijuana is a chronic problem and therefore of a more serious nature than the acute reac-

tions described above. When a person smokes marijuana two or three times daily, he accomplishes little else; there is just not enough time left for work. Measured against the large number of persons in the United States who smoke marijuana now and again without any impairment of their physical faculties or their ability to work or study, the number of potheads—those who are psychologically dependent on marijuana—must be very small, at least at the present time. Whether the number of potheads would increase if marijuana were legalized is something we cannot answer; certainly the possibility must be considered.

There are other bad reactions that have been ascribed to the use of marijuana and hashish:

1. *Hallucinations*   Although many drugs, such as LSD and mescaline, can cause hallucinations, marijuana and hashish do not, except upon occasion in response to an overdose. Cannabis products do enhance perceptions and can with high doses distort perceptions and disorganize spatial concepts. However, they are not known, when used by themselves, to bring on hallucinations in persons who have no prior history of psychosis or gross personality disorder.

2. *Psychosis*   Except for the rare occasion when suspiciousness and paranoia might linger for a few days, the evidence that marijuana or hashish can, in and of themselves, cause psychosis is very thin. The term *cannabis psychoses* has been used in parts of Asia and the Middle East as a general catchall diagnosis for a variety of mental disorders, but is now virtually discredited. In recent years one of us has talked with psychiatrists from India, Egypt, and Iraq and has also visited a large mental institution near Cairo. Two of the

psychiatrists interviewed had their training in England and were fairly convinced that the incidence and variety of serious mental disorders seen in their own hospitals was little different from that seen in public mental hospitals in England. The strongest statement that can be made in respect to psychosis is that hashish sometimes appears to be an aggravating factor in otherwise clearly defined mental disorders. The following quotation from the report, *"Cannabis,"* prepared by the British Government Advisory Committee on Drug Dependence in 1968, speaks to the questionable reliability of some official statistics on cannabis:

The diagnostic methods employed in many studies were, by any reasonable standard, woefully inadequate. In one large area, the diagnosis might be made by a policeman. The longstanding belief that cannabis caused insanity could strengthen this diagnosis in a doubtful case. Ingrained beliefs and habits are known to be powerful enemies of unbiased diagnosis.

3. *The flashback phenomenon* In certain circumstances marijuana or hashish can serve as a triggering mechanism that causes a return of symptoms, including hallucinations, experienced on an earlier LSD trip. Probably many bad experiences on marijuana are actually a combination of the direct action of cannabis with the symptoms of a return trip. It is often not possible, however, to obtain a clear history of past drug experience at the time of diagnosis.

To sum up

Marijuana can be described as a mildly intoxicating drug, best taken in congenial surroundings when the user does not anticipate physical or psychological demands.

Marijuana is not a narcotic.

It is not addictive; no physical craving develops for the drug, and no withdrawal symptoms appear when its use is stopped.

Marijuana does not give rise to tolerance.

It *is* habit forming, but the habit can be broken without difficulty, although often with regret.

For certain users, especially among youth, there *is* a risk of psychic dependence.

Marijuana causes no hangover.

It causes no lasting or irreversible damage to body or mind, as far as can be determined from present knowledge.

Mature marijuana leaves, each frond 8–10 inches long

Acid, mescaline, speed, and other drugs

In the early 1960s a group of new words and phrases burst into our language and consciousness. Hallucinogenic drugs—variously described as psychedelic, mind-manifesting, consciousness-expanding, or, more colloquially, mind-blowing—stirred our imagination. Foremost among this group of drugs was LSD, which quite suddenly became the most famous and the most infamous. In 1963 when a high school teacher in Illinois was told that his teenage son had been admitted to a hospital with an acute, severe mental disturbance following the ingestion of LSD, the father was bewildered. He did not know that such a drug existed. Today thousands and thousands of school teachers have some information about LSD stored in their minds and indeed would like more.

LSD is commonly termed *acid,* and for simplicity and clarity we will use the phrase "ingestion of LSD" interchangeably with "dropping acid," a phrase which had its origins in the illicit drug world but now has an established place in everyday language. The psychological experience

41

brought on by LSD—that strange journey of the mind—is called an acid trip. Through LSD a whole new world of possibilities for the human spirit at first appeared to be opening up, with promises of greater self-awareness, self-mastery, emotional fulfillment, diminished aggressiveness, and increased love—an ecstasy of the soul. To many, an acid trip was perceived as a profound religious experience, a transcendence over all those petty day-to-day practices and preoccupations that wear down the spirit. The taking of acid became a sacrament of sorts.

At the same time, frightening accounts of bad reactions to LSD began to appear in the press. We heard of the drug's horror, the terror and the nightmarish thoughts and feelings it inspired. Apparently those wonderful, liberating, transcendental experiences often turned out to be hells, which left a train of depression and morbid thought after the acute effects of the acid wore off. If some of these accounts were exaggerated, others were obviously true. Today there exists abundant evidence that LSD should not be taken except under the most carefully controlled of experimental situations.

In recent years hundreds of articles have been written on every conceivable aspect of LSD and its effects. Following is a history and a description of LSD—its effects and dangers—distilled from a review of available literature and from our own considerable observations, as clinicians who have interviewed and treated many young people who have taken LSD.

History of LSD

In 1938 Albert Hofmann, a Swiss research chemist working in the laboratories of a pharmaceutical company in Basel, performed a routine, experimental chemical synthesis. He brought together lysergic acid (which is found in ergot, a fungus or "rust" that grows on rye and wheat) and a diethylamide group, producing a new substance—d-lysergic acid diethylamide, or LSD 25. (The number *25* has no mysterious chemical significance, but merely tells us the date of the synthesis, the second day of May. If he had been working in the United States at the time, Dr. Hofmann might have named the substance LSD 52.) The extraordinary powers of this drug were not discovered until five years later when Dr. Hofmann accidentally ingested, by what route we do not know, a minute amount of LSD. Fortunately he kept a notebook in which he described the events that followed:

Last Friday, the 16 of April, I had to leave my work in the laboratory and go home because I felt strangely restless and dizzy. Once there, I lay down and sank into a not unpleasant delirium which was marked by an extreme degree of fantasy. In a sort of trance with closed eyes, fantastic visions of extraordinary vividness accompanied by a kaleidoscopic play of intense coloration continuously swirled around me. After two hours this condition subsided.

Suspecting a toxic cause, Hofmann went on to speculate:

On that Friday, however, the only unusual substances with which I had been in contact were d-lysergic acid and iso-lysergic acid diethylamide. (I had been trying various methods of purifying these isomers by condensation, and also breaking them down into their components.) In a preliminary experiment I had succeeded in producing a few milligrams of lysergic acid diethylamide as an easily soluble crystal in the form of a neutral tartrate. It was conceivable to me, however, that I could have absorbed enough of this material to produce the above described state. I was determined to probe the situation and I decided to experiment upon myself with a crystalline lysergic acid diethyla-

mide. If this material were really the cause, it must be active
in minute amounts, and I decided to begin with an extremely
small quantity.

Hofmann then took, by mouth, 250 micrograms of LSD.
After about forty minutes he noted "mild dizziness, restlessness, inability to concentrate, visual disturbance and uncon-
trollable laughter."

His diary continues:

At this point the entries in the laboratory notebook end. The
last words were written only with the greatest difficulty. I asked
my laboratory assistant to escort me home since I assumed that
the situation would progress in a manner similar to last Friday.
But on the way home (a four mile trip by bicycle), the symptoms developed with a much greater intensity than the first time.
I had the greatest difficulty speaking coherently and my field
of vision fluctuated and was distorted like the reflections in an
amusement park mirror. I also had the impression that I was
hardly moving, yet later my assistant told me that I was pedal-
ling at a fast pace. So far as I can recollect, the height of the
crisis was characterized by these symptoms; dizziness, visual distortions, the faces of those present appeared like grotesque colored masks, strong agitation alternating with paresis, the head,
body and extremities sometimes cold and numb; a metallic taste
on the tongue; throat dry and shriveled; a feeling of suffocation;
confusion alternating with a clear appreciation of the situation;
at times standing outside myself as a neutral observer and hearing myself muttering jargon or screaming half madly.

Six hours after taking the drug, my condition had improved.
The perceptual distortions were still present. Everything seemed
to undulate and their proportions were distorted like the reflections
on a choppy water surface. Everything was changing with unpleasant, predominantly poisonous green and blue color tones.
With closed eyes multi-hued, metamorphizing fantastic images
overwhelmed me. Especially noteworthy was the fact that sounds
were transposed into visual sensations so that from each tone or

noise a comparable colored picture was evoked, changing in form and color kaleidoscopically.

Hofmann apparently slept well and the next day felt "completely well, but tired."

Chemistry and pharmacology of LSD

LSD in its pure form is an odorless, tasteless, white crystalline powder, readily soluble in water. The drug does not alter the taste of any fluid in which it is dissolved. One remarkable property of LSD—a property that determined the discovery of its effects in such a dramatic way—is its enormous potency; doses of it can be measured in millionths of a gram, or micrograms. The average dose for dropping acid is two hundred micrograms, which means that one ounce of LSD can be split up into one hundred and fifty thousand doses.

These characteristics make control of the illicit manufacture and distribution of LSD virtually impossible. For example, a sheet of note paper can soak up a solution containing 1/500 of one ounce of LSD. After drying, this sheet of paper can be mailed from one country to another, for the price of an airmail stamp, with no fear of detection. Later the paper can be cut into three hundred squares, each containing two hundred micrograms of LSD. Such is not the usual way in which LSD is distributed, but the example indicates the enormous problems of control. Ordinarily LSD is sold either as a sugar cube in which a drop of a solution of LSD has been absorbed or in capsule or tablet form, with the LSD added to a carrying substance that in itself is, or should be, inert.

The potency of LSD raises many questions of a psycho-

45

pharmacological nature, for it is certain that only a minute amount of the LSD taken by mouth actually reaches the brain substance. Thus an amount of the drug so small that it can only be called molecular nevertheless has effects at several sites of action in the brain. Where these sites are and what the mechanism is that determines such profound psychological changes are unknown. There are many theories, but all of them are hypothetical and speculative. In order to understand what LSD does to the mind, what the events of a trip are like, and why the drug has inspired such extravagant claims, we must have some idea of the usual and ordinary train of events in the mind—what it means to perceive, to appreciate various things, to think, to weigh and assess alternatives, and in general to know and, at the same time, feel. The following is a brief description from a medical viewpoint of the brain and its functioning.

Perception

We perceive the world around us through our five senses. Outside stimuli cause vibrations of the eardrums; chemical changes in complex cells in the retina at the back of the eye, in the lining of the nose, and in the cells of the palate; and changes in the sensory nerve endings, which exist within the skin all over the body and in particular concentration in the fingertips. These reactions are translated or transformed into patterns of electrical impulses that travel to different parts of the brain. We have virtually no knowledge of what then takes place at various sites in the brain. We may, if we wish, be philosophical and wonder about the distortions and various message translations that have taken place between an event outside the body and the ultimate arrival of a given stimulus at a given site of action in the brain. Still, it is rather pointless to doubt that we do in fact see, hear, smell, taste, and touch. It should be emphasized, however, that what we actually perceive in our minds may only be a very rough approximation of what actually exists outside ourselves.

The outside world of things and events, which in large measure affects and determines our feelings and behavior, is commonly referred to as *reality*. Hence the definition that *reality* is what all of us share, all of us see and hear. "A rose is a rose is a rose" expresses a writer's way of emphasizing what we are trying to say. For example, one person might delight in growing roses while another might be repelled by an allergy to them, but they both agree that a rose is a rose. If, on the other hand, someone looking at a rose recoils in terror because he sees instead a horrifying, devouring monster, he has lost touch with reality and is having a delusion, maybe many at the same time. Experimental work has now established that for normal and ordinary psychological functioning, our five senses must feed a fairly constant stream of *percepts* (sensory input) to the brain. The intensity and variety of the percepts change greatly through the day, and obviously at different times one or another sense may receive virtually no messages, while others may be extremely active. If this stream of so-called stimuli or percepts is cut off experimentally, the subject is said to be in a state of sensory deprivation, and sooner or later, often within hours, he experiences considerable disorganization of thought and feeling. However, the subject remains aware that he is part of an experiment. Perhaps because of this awareness, he usually does not suffer marked anxiety, although he may become suspicious of, and indeed thoroughly paranoid toward, the person conducting the experiment. The main effect of sensory deprivation is that the subject enters a dreamlike state, characteristically a progressive sequence of visual hallucinations which resemble those of an acid trip. Auditory and other hallucinations are less common. The subject may, however, feel his body to be somehow alien, as if it were not his; he may even feel completely detached from his body, as if he were floating away from it and observing it from a distance. When sensory deprivation causes such symptoms to develop, the ability of the subject to perform tasks that require motor coordination or to do simple arithmetical tests is impaired, as is his judgment.

This strange state of mind has actually been sought after by many persons, who have found themselves in situations where suffering is continuous and intolerable and where the future appears to offer no hope or release. A former colleague, a surgeon, who was captured by the Japanese at the fall of Singapore, lived in a prison camp for four years. The conditions of the camp were grueling with extreme physical and mental privations. Settled into an arduous, timeless existence, almost devoid of hope, the prisoner could bring on feelings very like those we have just described by retiring to the bleakest, darkest, quietest corner of the camp, where he would squat and stare blankly into space. At times he was convinced that he was going mad, becoming schizophrenic, but nevertheless he deliberately brought on these spells or "trips" because they gave him substantial relief.

The *cognitive* function of the brain, or the sense of knowing, is the ability of the brain or mind to take those impressions perceived through the sense organs and do something with them, give them coherence—appreciate and understand them in terms of what is stored in memory, what is known from previous experiences. In this way, a uniquely human evaluative sense of knowing attaches itself to the particular

48

impulses perceived through the sense organs. The mind, so to speak, pulls together what the sense organs receive and applies the human ability to sort things out, place them in categories, and comprehend how they work or unfold.

Since the mind is not a concrete thing, but a flowing, everchanging invisible abstraction, what we are describing is not an objective or scientific description of brain functioning. It is no more than a mind's view of a mind. Perhaps that is all any of us can do, describe what is both miraculous and utterly prosaic, the way we think and recognize the world and make sense of it—and in so doing agree with one another that, for instance, leaves are green or sparrows have wings and are birds and can fly—and on and on.

Emotional functions in the brain and mind can be looked upon somewhat separately from the other functions. At all levels of perception and thought, *emotion* or *feeling* enters the neuro-psychological picture to greatly determine and mold the mind's train of events; just as emotion is reciprocally stirred by the cognitive and perceptive processes. The way in which emotions and more objective observations, or perceptions, mix or blend (words are sorely taxed at this point) varies from person to person. One person looks at a rose and is indifferently impassive, another blushes with pleasure, while yet another might recoil out of some idiosyncratic fear.

When they have a clear and understandable relationship to the thought processes, as they ordinarily do, emotions are described as appropriate. To be sad over a loss, to be depressed about an unfortunate event, to rage over an insult, to reach peaks of happiness and ecstasy because of another's love—all these are appropriate emotions. In mental disorders, such as schizophrenia and manic-depressive psychoses, emotions are less understandable. The afflicted person expresses emotions

49

that may seem appropriate to the situation as *he* sees it, but may not make sense to the outside observer in terms of the normal, shared concept of reality; thus, the emotion may be described as inappropriate.

Although we have some insight, however naive, into the progression from "outside events" to "evaluative knowing," we have virtually no understanding of what determines the translation of a thought or an emotion into action or behavior. Nor can we fail to acknowledge that what is called appropriate or inappropriate, or real or unreal, varies widely from society to society and even within societies.

The acid trip

There are in fact two ways of describing what acid does or the "acid trip." The first is laced with hyperbole, highly colored by the personality of the reporter, and strongly reminiscent of the most vivid dreams and nightmares. Some readers will have read such descriptions or at least fragments of them, and more are available in the recommended reading at the end of this book. The second, and the one we choose here, may seem by comparison more dull and prosaic. What we attempt to do is to describe the trip in terms that can convey more clearly the effects of the drug within the framework of the brain's workings, the mind's ways, as described above.

We cannot emphasize strongly enough the importance of the *set*—that combination of particular personality and mood of the user, and particular environment and circumstances in which the drug is taken—for it is the set that more or less determines the nature of the acid trip. Different persons, taking the same dose of LSD at the same time have vastly different trips;

indeed, the same person taking the same dose on separate occasions, can have one trip that he describes as ecstasy and another that he sees as a horrible nightmare. It *can* be stated generally, however, that the effects of ingesting three hundred micrograms of LSD—a usual dose—come on within one hour, peak in about two hours, and last for ten to sixteen hours, slowly subsiding.

Effects on perception

The sense of sight is the perceptual system most affected by LSD; external objects and sometimes people appear to undergo marked changes in color, shape, and perspective. Colors frequently become deeper, more vivid, intense, vibrant, and ephemeral. Yet they may reflect a user's somber mood by appearing gray and washed out, or his light mood by appearing bright and cheerful. Objects change their shapes and sizes, with the effect of the *Alice in Wonderland* phenomenon of shrinking and growing and with marked alterations in perspective. Objects often assume a different order of importance to the eye, so that ordinary things that we have ceased to notice may be suddenly invested with such newness and vividness that our attention focuses on them to the exclusion of more "interesting" items.

The effects described above are, strictly speaking, illusions; having taken LSD, the person perceives things differently from the way, in reality, they "are." Other common visual phenomena of the acid trip are changing, flowing, kaleidoscopic patterns, geometric and colorful, that move across the visual field. Because they are more likely to occur when the eyes are closed, these patterns appear to stem from the effect of the acid on the cells of the retina. The use of LSD also brings on hallucinations, which should be distinguished from illusions, even though the terms have become almost interchangeable in common usage. A hallucination is something seen outside oneself that in reality is not there. In addition to visual hallucinations, there are hallucinations of sound, taste, smell, and touch. The hallucinations on an acid trip are more often than not "pseudo-hallucinations," for the subject may be aware that his perceptions are not grounded in reality. He does not believe in them as do persons hallucinating from psychological disorders, such as schizophrenia, or experiencing the acute withdrawal syndrome of the chronic alcoholic (more commonly known as the DTs).

Changes in the other sense perceptions caused by LSD are minor compared with the visual ones. Hearing can be more intense and touch more sensitive, although the increased sensitivity is sometimes accompanied by an uncomfortable numbness and tingling of the hands and feet. Taste and smell may be enhanced, but this is not common.

Another strange phenomenon termed *synesthesia* is frequently experienced on an LSD trip. When synesthesia takes place, the different sensory pathways through the brain seem to become crossed, interfering with and enhancing one another. Sounds received by the ear may evoke visual imagery; that is, auditory stimuli may be "seen," and likewise a visual impulse entering the brain may be "heard" or even "smelled" and "felt."

LSD strangely alters the effect of time. Moments seem like an eternity, and a perception "becomes frozen in an infinity of experiences." The present drowns out the past and the future. On the whole, for most trips, time appears to slow down, while thoughts and feelings tumble through the mind in great profusion. Time can also appear to go into reverse; for example, the subject might have the odd sensation of drinking a cup of tea before it is actually brewed, and of brewing it before the idea of drinking tea has even crossed his mind. In his own way, Lewis Carroll in *Through the Looking-Glass* has described this effect:

"I don't understand you," said Alice. "It's dreadfully confusing!"

"That's the effect of living backwards," the Queen said kindly: "it always makes one a little giddy at first—"

"Living backwards!" Alice repeated in great astonishment. "I never heard of such a thing!"

"—but there's one great advantage in it, that one's memory works both ways."

"I'm sure *mine* only works one way," Alice remarked. "I can't remember things before they happen."

"It's a poor sort of memory that only works backwards," the Queen remarked.

"What sort of things do *you* remember best?" Alice ventured to ask.

"Oh, things that happened the week after next," the Queen replied in a careless tone. "For instance, now" she went on, . . . "there's the King's Messenger. He's in prison now, being punished: and the trial doesn't even begin till next Wednesday: and of course the crime comes last of all."

The hallucinations experienced on an acid trip clearly have to do with perception, knowing, and feeling. And it is at this point in the description of an acid trip that language frequently becomes inadequate, for there is no clear-cut vocabulary with which to examine hallucinations. "We are," says Prospero, "such stuff as dreams are made on." A hallucination to one man can be a malevolent spirit, to another a toxic symptom, and to yet another a religious experience. The hallucinations brought on by LSD are rarely devoid of feeling and

53

meaning to the subject. The hallucinated images sometimes represent things and people from his own life, often dredged from a distant past; at other times they are the work of a somewhat feverish, jolted, stimulated imagination. They may be pleasing or frightening, aesthetically satisfying or drab.

Effects on knowing and feeling

When those who have taken LSD describe an acid trip, superlatives abound and the experience seems intrinsically incommunicable. The rich insights, the sense of "knowing," the oneness with the universe, and the communion with an "absolute" are all tantalizing expressions of effects or "events" in the deepest recesses of the mind. But these effects, clearly considered worthwhile by those who describe them, remain curiously ineffable. Upon reading Aldous Huxley's eloquent account of experiences with mescaline in *The Doors of Perception,* one is left strangely unsatisfied. Although fascinating, the book provides no contagion of ecstasy to the reader. One is left with the message that a trip itself, whether on LSD or mescaline, offers the only route to discovering what Huxley and others have found.

Christopher Mayhew, a member of the British House of Commons, wrote a letter to the *London Times* describing an early "psychedelic experience" in the middle 1950s, when he had taken "an LSD-type hallucinogenic drug" to test a theory:

I experienced the beatific vision, eternal life, heaven. It was all there as the saints had described it—ecstasy, timelessness, illumination and unity, or, if you prefer it, depersonalization, time disturbances, light hallucinations and the disintegration of the ego.

54

Dangers of LSD

A bad trip on LSD is not in itself necessarily dangerous. The subject may suffer frightful torments of the mind during a trip, yet emerge from it apparently unscathed. A serious problem, however, is that of death by accident. While on a trip, for example, a person might no longer feel bound by the laws of gravity and so impulsively walk through an open window —expecting, no doubt, to float in mid-air or drift gently to the ground. Or he might weave across a busy street, believing that a kind of "two-dimensionality," as it has been called, prevents him from being squashed by rushing cars. To prevent such accidents, some LSD users take trips only if accompanied by someone who remains "clean," or undrugged. The undrugged person is known as the "guide," "protector," "shepherd," or "shepherdess."

The return trip or flashback

The strange and frightening phenomenon of the return trip —the sudden return of the symptoms of a trip, despite the fact that no LSD has been taken in the interval—is well documented. The flashback can occur within days or weeks, but sometimes not for many months, and mild flashbacks have taken place as long as sixteen months after the ingestion of LSD. The return trip appears more commonly after LSD has been taken several times, but can also occur after a single trip. The triggering mechanism apparently is some form of stress, such as exhaustion, irritability, a fever, or even a bad cold; and *smoking marijuana can also bring on a return trip*. The symptoms are usually milder and of much shorter duration than those

55

originally experienced and frequently, but not always, resemble them closely. On the whole, the surprise and shock precipitated by the awareness that a flashback has begun cause more alarm than the return trip itself; but sometimes a return trip in itself generates more anxiety and more vivid imagery than the original.

How common return trips are no one really knows. A very rough guess is that 20 percent of those who have "tripped" three or more times are likely to experience return trips; but why some have many such flashbacks and others only one is a mystery. It is possible that after taking LSD a specific "triggering threshold" for a return of the symptoms persists in diminishing degree for perhaps two years, so that if stress is great enough during that time, the subject would experience the flashback phenomenon.

The flashback may occur once or several times during a period of several months, usually with diminishing intensity, but occasionally of a different pattern. One man who had dropped acid at least thirty times within about three years would, as he put it, "flip in and out" several times each day. He had to make elaborate plans so that, while at work, he could inconspicuously remove himself from the presence of others for the brief periods of flashbacks. For almost one year—with the symptoms gradually fading—he lived that way, plagued and in fear. Specific drug treatments that usually prove effective in neutralizing return trips had little, if any, effect.

An even more unusual case history raises some fascinating and disturbing questions. A twenty-year-old man, well educated and intelligent, with a healthy measure of cynicism in his view of the world, had smoked marijuana several times with what he felt to be entirely pleasurable and satisfactory results. For some time he had toyed with the idea of taking LSD, and indeed his curiosity had led him to read more widely about acid than do most young people before trying it. In tranquil surroundings and in the presence of a friend who did not take the drug, he swallowed three hundred micrograms of LSD and experienced what he believed was a good trip. During the several hours of the trip there were moments when he was vaguely frightened, but his friend was there to touch him and reassure him, and in the main he described his experiences in the usual vague, glowing terms, but with comparatively reserved enthusiasm. He sensed in a strange incommunicable sort of way that he had seen more deeply "into his life" than ever before, but was not eager to repeat the experience, although he expressed no regrets. By the next day he was apparently his normal self again.

Approximately two months later, while changing a tire on his car, he slipped and struck his head sharply in the region of the left temple. Within a few minutes he was experiencing a flashback, or return trip. The symptoms were more or less like the original ones, except that they were more frightening with rapidly changing visual disturbances, including visual hallucinations that he described as strident and of a dark and horrifying nature. The visual hallucinations also had a strange auditory component, experienced as fearful and threatening, but hard to pin down in words. He said he felt "the stench of death."

Under medical care within several hours, he was treated with chlorpromazine, a drug usually very effective in toning down the intensity of flashback hallucinations and in diminishing the fears of a return trip. However, chlorpromazine failed to work, and the return trip continued with varying, but on the whole undiminished, intensity for several days. Because of certain similarities between his symptoms and those often seen in temporal lobe epilepsy (a condition marked by episodic bursts, or fits, of hyperactivity in one of the temporal lobes of the brain) at this time he was given an anti-epileptic drug. Within a few days all his symptoms had subsided, and after four weeks of treatment the medication was stopped. One week later his symptoms returned, so once more he was given anti-epileptic medication with the same good result. Six months later the medication was gradually reduced and then stopped, and he has since been free of symptoms.

The parallel between the LSD-related symptoms in the above case and the symptoms of epilepsy can be appreciated further after a description of the so-called supernova experience, a common "happening" during an acid trip. The supernova experience might be described as "a great burst of all-illuminating energy" and startling intensity that "transports" or gives insight and, often enough, brings fear and bewilderment. Compare this with the reflections of Prince Myshkin in Dostoyevsky's novel, *The Idiot*. (Dostoyevsky himself was an epileptic.)

. . . there was a moment or two in his epileptic condition almost before the fit itself . . . when suddenly amid the sadness, spiritual darkness and depression, his brain seemed to catch fire at brief moments, and with an extraordinary momentum his vital forces were strained to the utmost all at once. His sensation of being alive and his awareness increased tenfold at those moments which flashed by like lightning. His mind and heart were flooded by a dazzling light. All his agitation, all his doubts and worries, seemed composed in a twinkling, culminating in a great calm, full of serene and harmonious joy and hope, full of understanding and the knowledge of the final cause. But those moments, those flashes of intuition, were merely the presentiment of the last second (never more than a second) which preceded the actual fit . . . Reflecting about that moment afterwards, when he was well again, he often said to himself that all those gleams and flashes of the highest awareness and, hence, also of "the highest mode of existence," were nothing but a disease, a departure from the normal condition, and, if so, it was not at all the highest mode of existence, but, on the contrary, must be considered to be the lowest. And yet he arrived at last at the paradoxical conclusion: "What if it is a disease?" he decided at last. "What does it matter that it is an abnormal tension, if the result, if the moment of sensation, remembered and analysed in a state of health, turns out to be harmony and beauty brought to their highest point of perfection, and gives a feeling, undivined and undreamt of till then, of completeness, proportion, reconciliation, and an ecstatic and prayerful fusion in the highest synthesis of life?" . . . He could reason sanely about it when the attack was over and he was well again. Those moments were merely an intense heightening of awareness—if this condition had to be expressed in one word—of awareness and at the same time of the most direct sensation of one's own existence to the most intense degree. If in that second—that is to say, at the last conscious moment before the fit—he had time to say to himself, consciously and clearly, "Yes, I could give my whole life for this moment," then this moment by itself was, of course, worth the whole of life. However, he did not insist on the dialectical part of his argument: stupor, spiritual darkness, idiocy stood before him as the plain consequence of those "highest moments.". . . What indeed was he to make of this reality? . . . He *had* had time to say to himself at the particular second that, for the infinite happiness he had felt in it, it might well be worth the whole of his life. "At that moment . . . the extraordinary saying that *there shall be time no longer* becomes, somehow, comprehensible to me."

Turning back to our patient, what are we to say about this man's experiences—what happened within his brain? Assuming, as we must, that the LSD had been excreted from his body long before the return trip, there seems one likely, but frightening, explanation: the LSD may have caused a chemical lesion in his brain, probably in one or the other temporal lobe. Even if there were no other reason for being extremely cautious about the use of LSD, this case history alone should give pause. And we must also be concerned with the possibility that the presumed brain lesion might cause other, more subtle, changes to the personality of the user—changes not immediately evident either to him or to others.

Diminished capacity for abstract thinking and creative work

There is some evidence that an insidious consequence of dropping acid is that the mind becomes dulled and dazed. This does not happen to everyone who takes LSD, but it does occur and has been observed. Three years ago a small group of young scientists, all intelligent and creative men, decided to try LSD to learn how, if at all, their ability to formulate and manipulate abstract concepts might be altered. The expectation, by the way, was that such ability might improve, but the exact opposite proved true. The men had no particular problems with the trip itself; on the whole, they felt it to be an exciting and wonderful adventure of the mind. But for seven or eight months afterward, each subject discovered his ability to think creatively at a high level of abstraction and to design complex research experiments was significantly impaired. The scientists were quite able to carry on formal teaching functions and were able to go about their work without alarming or worrying their colleagues in any way. Still, almost a full year went by before *they* felt they were absolutely back to normal —and they were men *favorably* disposed toward LSD when they took it.

Psychosis

A psychosis is a serious mental disorder characterized by disorganization of the personality with fragmentation of thoughts and feelings and commonly with delusions and hallucinations. For convenience, psychoses are divided according to presumed cause into three categories: organic, toxic, and unknown.

An *organic psychosis,* for example, can arise from a brain tumor or degenerative changes secondary to old age. There is actual physical destruction of certain parts of the brain, which means normal thought processes are disrupted. The flashback phenomena experienced after LSD trips can be considered an episodic psychosis caused by organic change. If the brain of an LSD user were examined, lesions perhaps would not be visible to the naked eye or even through the microscope, but it is reasonable to assume that if the molecular structure of the brain could be seen, an abnormal pattern or lesion would be found.

Strictly speaking, however, the acute symptoms of an acid trip represent a *toxic psychosis*—that is to say, symptoms usually considered psychotic have been brought on by the ingestion of a substance, LSD, that has proved toxic to the brain. Many who have taken LSD and are convinced that the experience was good, lasting, and therefore worthwhile might take exception to the representation of a trip as an acute toxic psychosis. Yet, the behavioral impairment during a trip certainly indicates that representation.

The category of psychoses classified as *of unknown cause* includes schizophrenia and manic-depressive states. There are now many cases on record of the development of psychosis following hard on the heels of an acid trip. The reasons for this are, again, unknown. Some who have wished to play down the possible dangers of LSD claim that a psychosis is precipitated only if a "pre-psychotic state" existed before acid was taken. Whatever a "pre-psychotic state" is, and we consider it a dubious phrase, such argument can be of no comfort to a victim who might well have stayed "pre-psychotic" (others might say "normal") until the age of ninety-five. As a matter of fact, the psychotic symptoms that often enough follow an acid trip closely resemble—indeed are indistinguishable from—those present in schizophrenia. At other times the psychosis, although having some features in common with schizophrenia, appears to have a pattern different from that found in schizophrenia. The LSD psychosis may be of relatively brief duration, but some psychotic illnesses closely following the ingestion of LSD have lasted more than one year. The following case history illustrates this.

A nineteen-year-old girl decided to celebrate her boyfriend's twenty-second birthday by taking acid with him. It was her first such experience, and his third. They were cautious enough to insist on the presence of the man's roommate, a youth who had also taken acid trips, but this time stayed "clean" to act as the "shepherd."

For the man the trip was a good one, not much different from his earlier experiences; and within eight to ten hours he was apparently his normal self again. The girl also had what appeared to be a good trip, although the vividness of her visions and the inconstancy of the images unnerved her and gave her a great feeling of insecurity. However, as is often the case, she was soothed by the reassurances and closeness of friends. At no time did she appear terrified or become paranoid. As she emerged slowly from the trip and for several hours afterwards, she expressed both satisfaction with the experience and the conviction that she had achieved a newer and more profound level of appreciation—both of herself as a person and of the relationship between her and her boyfriend. Approximately twenty hours after taking LSD, however, she quite suddenly became extremely fearful of her boyfriend, thinking that he was about to kill her. In another twenty-four hours she was floridly psychotic, her symptoms now indistinguishable from paranoid schizophrenia.

During the next five days her symptoms rapidly melted away. During that time she was in a hospital, however, and almost constantly in the presence of persons she knew well and had always liked. At the same time she was treated with a phenothiazine drug that has proved very effective in paranoid illnesses. Within one week she had apparently regained her normal mental state, but her manner was subdued. Her medication was slowly reduced and then, after another two weeks, stopped. Her spirits seemed normal. Approximately two weeks later, within a space of several hours, she plunged into a profound depression with severe agitation. In spite of constant attention she attempted suicide by slashing her wrists, but fortunately escaped serious injury. Another two months elapsed before the depression finally gave way. Four years later she appeared "normal" in every respect except one. She had a single delusion that waxed and waned: she was convinced that her brain was rotting and visited innumerable doctors to request that tests be taken. She was, however, able to work and function normally, and apparently the delusion was beginning to fade.

To comment on this case is only to confess bewilderment. The life history of this young woman prior to dropping acid gave no indication that she would be particularly vulnerable to LSD. By no stretch of the imagination could she have been labeled pre-psychotic (a term, in any event, that has little meaning). The *set* was good—at least it appeared so by every measure. One is left in the dark. One is also left to worry, seriously worry about anyone who takes LSD.

Genetic damage

In March 1967 Maimon Cohen, a geneticist, reported that when white blood cells grown in culture media outside the body are exposed to LSD, changes occur in the chromosomes (carriers of heredity contained in every human cell; the blueprints for reproduction). This discovery raised a serious question of the possible effects of LSD on the genetic makeup of the user and particularly on the growing fetus if the user takes LSD when pregnant. The use of thalidomide—with its consequences, the birth of thousands of deformed children—had prompted scientists to observe more carefully than ever before the chromosomal changes in persons exposed to new drugs, and so, naturally, Dr. Cohen's report sounded a widespread alarm. Much research on the chromosomes of LSD users has been done since then, and it now appears to be well established that the percentage of "damaged" or "broken" chromosomes is higher in LSD users than in non-users. Also, a number of clinical reports have documented spontaneous abortions and birth of deformed babies to women who had taken LSD during early pregnancy.

Yet, recently, scientists have begun to wonder for the following reasons whether, after all, LSD does cause such genetic damage: 1. It is not at all statistically certain that women who have used LSD give birth to a higher proportion of ab-

64

normal children.* 2. The significance of chromosomal "breaks" is far from being completely understood, but it is known that they cannot be equated simply with genetic damage. 3. Many other substances that are apparently innocuous are now known to cause chromosomal "breaks," and the number of "abnormal" chromosomes in the white blood cells increases markedly during illnesses such as influenza.

Nevertheless, the danger of genetic damage is not to be dismissed; that is, it cannot yet be denied that LSD users may indeed have a greater likelihood than others of producing damaged children. A mother who has taken LSD and then given birth to such a child will certainly get no comfort from the outcome, one way or the other, of such a controversy. Although there is no incontrovertible evidence at the moment that genetic damage results from LSD, there *is* enough evidence to establish such a possibility—perhaps enough presumptive evidence to suggest that it is very unwise to take LSD during pregnancy or, for that matter, throughout the reproductive years.

Other hallucinogenic drugs

The very idea of mind-altering drugs is a relatively new one for most people in the Western world. About two thousand years ago, under the influence of philosophers such as Plato

* As this book goes to press, we learn from Dr. Cecil B. Jacobson, a geneticist at George Washington University, that a long-term and continuing study in Washington is producing strong evidence that women who have taken LSD during early pregnancy, *or even before the time of conception,* run a significantly higher risk of giving birth to abnormal babies, some with very gross deformities, than a comparable group of women who have not taken LSD.

and Aristotle, Western thought took a sharp turn away from paganism and towards rationalism. The earlier paganism of the Greeks and the Romans allowed for a much easier blending of religious, mystical, and so-called worldly feelings; fantasies wove in and out of what is now termed *reality*. The pagan gods, though immortal, were human in their vices and loves and joys and failings; like man, they could be vengeful and petty and petulant. Gods mixed closely with men, and men with their gods. The influence of Aristotelian philosophy and logic shifted the whole tenor and balance of Western thought. A "duality of being" emerged, in which the "inner-mystical-religious-imaginative self" was separate from reason and intellect. Western civilization became more and more concerned with physical explanations and mastery of the natural world; religious and mystical preoccupations gradually became less and less commanding. Late in the seventeenth century, when Newton exclaimed, "Oh, God, I think thy thoughts after thee" he meant that he and other scientists could delve into the corners of all creation, until then the divine province of God, and describe an intelligible, law-abiding physical system.

Newton, however, did not discard the idea that the universe should be known through the greater glory of God. In point of fact, later in his life Newton became more and more preoccupied with religion and mysticism. But present day scientists do not need religion or mysticism to come to terms with their knowledge. Most of them believe that rational explanations of natural phenomena are no more than beautiful constructs or theories, suspended in an abstraction called the cosmos—and the cosmos is, by definition, beyond the complete comprehension of man.

In 1902 William James took gentle issue with the accepted "duality of being" in a series of lectures subsequently published as a book, *The Varieties of Religious Experience*. He described with great sensitivity the events in the life of the mind when, in mystical ways, the inner imagination fuses with outer reality to reveal new and deeper insights, which are clearly felt but cannot easily be communicated to others. One happy consequence of our "psychedelic age" is that his excellent book, probably little read twenty years ago, is now much in demand. Neither in Asia and the subcontinent of India nor among the indigenous Indian population of America has an Aristotle risen to such a position of influence, or a Newton— for reasons both too obvious and too complicated to discuss here. The fine blend of mysticism, religion, and science that characterizes the practice of "traditional" medicine in India is usually very confusing to Westerners, and no wonder that is so. In the East various herbs or drugs are used to produce intensified, dreamlike, or transcendental states of mind—a tradition of long standing. Westerners have no such influential tradition alive at the present time, certainly not in America's suburbs.

Peyote, mescal, and mescaline

For many American Indians the ritual use of mescal, or peyote, has long been a part of their culture and religion. Before 1890 the use of peyote was confined to the Indian tribes who lived in the region of the Rio Grande valley; after that the cult spread rapidly among other Indian tribes, to include the Sioux and Chippewa in the North and the Ute in the West. Among some tribal groups the new peyote ritual became interwoven with the new Christianity—probably a desperate attempt on the part of the Indians to maintain freedom of the soul and racial identity after their decimation by white settlers.

The peyote cactus (the word *peyote* derives from the Aztec *peyotl*), botanical name *lophophora Williamsii,* grows with ease in northern Mexico and north of the Rio Grande. The buds from the cactus are cut off and dried, after which they shrink to hard button-shaped discs up to two inches in diameter. These are called mescal buttons or, to Indians who use them, "holy food" from the "divine plant" (the word *mescal* can be confusing because it is also the name given to a popular Mexican alcoholic drink). The mescal buttons, thinly sliced or shredded, can either be chewed and eaten or brewed to make an active "tea." (The ritual use of peyote in the United States is legal for members of the Native American Church.)

The active ingredient of the peyote button has been synthesized and given the name *mescaline.* In the illicit world of drugs, peyote is usually supplied chopped or ground in gelatin capsules, pressed into pellets, or liquified in ampules. The buttons are sometimes called "moons" or, if large, "full moons." Mescaline is sold as a fine crystalline powder in gelatin capsules or as a liquid in ampules.

Effects of mescaline

As with drugs previously discussed, the *set* is an important factor in determining the experience of taking peyote. Thus, when peyote is taken openly as part of a social and religious ritual, the effects are fairly constant and predictable; when it is taken illicitly in secretive surroundings, the effects are much less predictable, and acute anxiety and panic reactions are not uncommon.

When the shredded button is ingested, the user will sometimes feel nausea and vomit; if the vomiting occurs early, no other symptoms may develop. William James tried peyote and

68

wrote his brother Henry, "I took one bud three days ago, was violently sick for twenty-four hours, and had no other symptoms whatever . . . I will take the visions on trust!" Visual effects, which tend to dominate the peyote experience, begin within about thirty to forty-five minutes, reach a peak within one to two hours, and then slowly subside over a period of ten to twelve hours. Visual perceptions are markedly distorted. Objects take on more vivid, vibrant, and intense qualities with heightened color and a fluidity or plasticity of form, which makes them seem to change their shape or color, often quite rapidly. Objects undergo transformations in size and perspective; they shrink one minute, enlarge the next—now recede, now come close. For a small number of peyote subjects, a particular thought can manage to influence the nature and variety of the distorted perceptions. Visual hallucinations are commonly experienced—that is to say, visual images are sparked in the brain without relation to outside objects. Particular visual hallucinations frequently recur; typically, they are colored geometric shapes. (Heinrich Klüver in 1928 called them "form-constants.")

The peyote user is aware that the distortions and hallucinations are induced by the drug. He usually has the ability to step back from the symptoms and ground himself in reality with much greater ease than is possible on an acid trip. Although changes in the other sense perceptions are much less common, distortions and hallucinations of taste, smell, sound, and touch do occur.

Synesthesia, or the crossing over of one sensory perception to another, is common; as with LSD, for example, sounds may be "seen" and outside visual stimuli may be "heard" or "felt" as well as seen. The throbbing of a drum or any repetitive beat can enhance the variety and richness of visions. One observer described each audible stroke of a pendulum as an "explosion of colors." As with LSD, the sense of time becomes infinitely elastic, and the perception of an event stretches through eternity or hovers in a perpetual moment.

Turning to the effects of peyote on cognition, or "knowing," and mood, there is, once again, marked similarity to the LSD experience. In 1928 Heinrich Klüver coined the term *presque vu* (almost seen) to describe a strange feeling commonly experienced under the influence of mescal and other hallucinogens—a sense of being on the verge of a great insight, an apocalyptic revelation, or an incontrovertible truth. The subject's mood is typically somewhat euphoric; laughter comes easily and may continue beyond the initial provocation of mirth. For some, the mood may be contemplative or mildly depressive.

The dangers of mescaline are slight when compared to LSD. If the *set* is poor, taking the drug may be a very unpleasant experience, occasionally causing panic and depression, and a sense of detachment and uneasiness may linger for several days.

Psilocybin and other naturally occurring hallucinogens

There are more than forty known species of plants growing on the American continent that can produce visions—distortions of visual perceptions with or without visual hallucinations. Wild mushrooms, so abundant in variety, have been found to possess an astonishing range of potent chemicals. At one end of the scale is the lethal, crimson-spotted mushroom, *amanita muscarina,* while at the other is the edible and delicious field mushroom. In between are many varieties that contain psychoactive substances such as psilocybin, found in the Mexican mushroom, *psilocybe mexicana.*

70

Like peyote, mushrooms are taken in religious ceremonies by many Indians of Mexico. (As far as is known, *psilocybe mexicana* was in use long before the flourishing of the Aztec civilization and was called teonanacatl, or "God's flesh.") The effects of psilocybin last three to four hours and have the same general characteristics, although usually milder, as those of peyote.

Of the other plants containing psychoactive drugs, we will mention only two—the Hawaiian wood rose and the morning glory. Around 1966 the seeds of the Hawaiian wood rose enjoyed a short-lived popularity as an hallucinogenic drug. The dried hips of the wood rose are quite beautiful and have long been used for Christmas decorations. Each of the hips contains four seeds, eight to twelve of which, when swallowed, can cause effects similar to, but much shorter than, an acid trip. One of the substances in this seed is LSA, lysergic acid amide, a close relative to LSD. Fortunately, Hawaiian wood rose seeds induce severe nausea and occasionally violent vomiting.

Morning glory seeds contain several substances closely related to LSD, and they, too, can cause severe nausea. The effects are variable, but much the same as those experienced after taking Hawaiian wood rose seeds. With large doses of the seeds of either plant, return trips can occur and, in any case, symptoms of anxiety and fear often persist for a day or two.

A second generation of synthetic hallucinogens

During the 1960s several new synthetic substances found their way to the illicit drug market. Most prominent among them are DMT, STP, and MDA.

DMT, or dimethyltryptamine, is closely related chemi-

71

cally to psilocybin. Although it is probably without effect if taken by mouth, some claim to have experienced mild, short-lived, dreamlike states. In assessing such reports, it must be remembered that anticipation and expectation are important influences in determining states of mind. When DMT is smoked, the effects most closely resemble those of an LSD trip, but are much milder, usually lasting no more than two hours. The possible dangers of taking DMT have not been clearly established, but recurring anxiety attacks for one to two weeks afterwards have been reported.

The commercial name *STP* (actually a gasoline additive that supposedly can do remarkable things for the power of an automobile motor) has been borrowed by drug takers to designate a chemical (DOM) synthesized by the Dow Chemical Company. Users of illicit drugs, bound neither by definitions nor convention, with a mixture of cavalier ignorance and carelessness refer to several different substances as STP. DOM bears a close chemical relationship to mescaline, and its effects on the user are somewhere between those of LSD and mescaline.

MDA or methylene dioxy-amphetamine, is a synthetic drug that appeared early in 1969. Although MDA is usually taken by mouth, there are subjective reports indicating that some of its effects can be brought on by smoking oregano or marijuana on which the powdered drug has been sprinkled. Descriptions of the effects by those who claim to have taken the drug, however, are at great variance. Tentatively, it can be stated that MDA causes moderate euphoria with vivid intensification of visual perception and frequent impairment of depth perception.

MDA has been called the "love drug" for reasons that are not clear, although one male user described the bodily experience brought on by the drug as "like a two-hour orgasm." Feelings of terror under the influence of MDA appear to be

72

common, but suspiciousness and paranoia are unusual. The effects of the drug wear off in three to six hours, but depression and inability to concentrate frequently follow and may last for several days. Some who have taken LSD and MDA at different times feel that MDA is more to be avoided, because its terror is more difficult to shake off and does not respond so readily to reassurance and touch, even when the *set* in every way appears right. Long-term effects and dangers, if any, of MDA are not known.

Speed

Methamphetamine hydrochloride, or *speed,* is a drug commonly taken for its ability to suppress appetite and to elevate mood. It belongs to a large group of drugs called amphetamines, which are prescribed far too frequently for weight reduction, for fighting depression, for warding off sleep, and for speeding up mental activity. In 1969 the Swedish government banned the manufacture, distribution, and prescription of amphetamines because of careless use and massive abuse; the dangers of this group of drugs were clearly seen to outweigh its value. Unfortunately, amphetamines are legally prescribed by the hundreds of millions each year in the United States and probably as many or more find their way into the illicit drug market.

An individual can build up an enormous tolerance to speed in a very short space of time. The methedrine user, or "speed freak," who injects huge doses of the drug directly into his blood stream, experiences two effects. The immediate effect, the "rush," is a feeling of exhilaration and of the blood pounding through the body, especially in the head. This subsides within minutes and is followed by the "high"—a flood of physi-

73

cal and mental energy, often poorly coordinated and accompanied by euphoria. After two to four hours a "down" comes, when the subject feels weak, exhausted, and often depressed. Speed is not addictive—it does not cause withdrawal symptoms or physical craving—but psychological and physical dependence can be serious problems.

Dangers of speed

An immediate danger of speed is sudden death during the "rush"; this is rare, but it does happen. The probable cause is that the heart increases its beat to such a rapid rate that it begins to quiver, thereafter ceasing to work as a pump. Death follows from lack of oxygen to the brain. A more chronic and frequent danger to the "speed freak" is the rapid exhaustion of his mental and physical reserves. He loses weight, becomes aggressively irritable, and sleeps very little. Acute toxic psychosis is not uncommon, with hallucinations, paranoid symptoms, and outbursts of irrational, aggressive, and sometimes violent behavior. Death can result from a combination of malnutrition and toxic exhaustion of the brain.

Another possible complication of methedrine is hepatitis (a viral inflammation of the liver) which can be caused by the use of contaminated syringes or needles. Although usually mild, this form of hepatitis has a tendency to relapse; in addition, there is always the possibility of permanent damage to the liver.

Sniffing glue and other volatile hydrocarbons

A practice mainly confined to younger adolescents is sniffing fumes from airplane glue and other volatile hydrocarbons, in-

74

cluding gasoline, aerosol propellants, dry-cleaning fluids, and paint thinner. The effects of this practice are enormously varied, ranging from dizziness to euphoria, to other-worldliness, to distortion of visual images, to headaches and vomiting. Some of these substances can be extremely damaging to body tissues—the brain, liver, and kidneys—and can depress the ability of the bone marrow to manufacture blood. Depending on the dosage, damage may be temporary or permanent, and many youngsters have died from acute poisoning.

Sniffing chemical fumes is not altogether a new phenomenon. Many years ago Oliver Wendell Holmes, a famous American physician and jurist, wrote down the inspiration that had come to him while under the influence of ether:

The veil of eternity was lifted. The one great truth, that which underlies all human experience, and is the key to all mysteries that philosophy has sought in vain to solve, flashed upon me in a sudden revelation. Henceforth all was clear: a few words had lifted my intelligence to the level of the knowledge of the cherubim. As my natural condition returned, I remembered my resolution and staggered to my desk. I wrote, in ill-shaped, straggling characters, the all-embracing truth still glimmering in my consciousness. The words were these (children may smile; the wise will ponder) : "A strong smell of turpentine prevails throughout."

A look to the future

The drugs described in this chapter are all potentially dangerous in greater or lesser degree and will therefore probably become obsolete as other less harmful drugs are synthesized or discovered. It should be remembered that the earliest of the sulphonamide drugs, M&B 693 ("that admirable M&B" Winston Churchill called it after his recovery from a serious attack of pneumonia during World War II), was very toxic; never-

75

theless it often saved lives when severe fulminating infections threatened to overwhelm natural body defenses and could not be controlled in any other way. After other less toxic sulphonamide drugs were developed, M&B 693 dropped from the scene.

More than 90 percent of the scientists *who ever lived* are alive today, and the volume of research in the fields of physiology, biochemistry, and pharmacology is staggering. The number of new substances that can be synthesized and tested for potential use on human beings is limitless. What, then, is to happen if drugs are developed which can induce all of the pleasurable symptoms, or the profound insights and other desirable effects claimed for the acid trip without any of the unpleasant ones and without dangerous consequences? Such drugs are bound to present us with serious moral dilemmas—dilemmas surely worth pondering now.

Peyote cactus buds

| Heroin

The drug scene, constantly changing, has taken a particularly dramatic and dangerous turn in recent months. As we scan our newspapers each day, early in this first spring of the new decade, we learn that heroin, not long ago considered a drug of the black ghetto and perhaps for that reason largely ignored by middle class suburban communities, has now spilled across racial, class, and town boundaries. But the problem is not new to some Americans. *In the first few months of 1951, no less than 260 boys and girls, their ages ranging from fourteen to twenty, were admitted to Bellevue Hospital in New York City because of addiction to heroin. Other children were killed by the drug and never made it to the hospital. They were all from Harlem and they made no headlines in the New York papers, let alone those in Boston or Seattle.*

What has now become clear is that 1. heroin is more readily obtainable in the large city suburbs than ever before; 2. there are now willing pushers operating either directly or indirectly in these suburbs; 3. there is clearly a psychological readiness among many young people, far removed socially, economically, and in spirit from the ghetto, to reach out and use heroin; and 4. there is appalling ignorance of the effects and dangers of heroin among these same young people.

In a later chapter some possible reasons for this "psychological readiness" are discussed. Here we will say only that the laws themselves tragically fail to discriminate adequately between the nature and the relative dangers of marijuana and heroin, all of which makes for confusion in the minds of the young and loss of confidence in those who all too often apply these laws in arbitrary—more usually called discretionary—fashion.

What is heroin? Where does it come from?

Heroin, as noted earlier, is a chemical substance derived from morphine. Morphine (after Morpheus, the name given by Ovid to the god of dreams, the son of Sleep) is one of a group of chemicals called alkaloids that are found in opium; and opium is obtained from the poppy plant. The simple and rather beautiful poppy flower gives way to a seed pod which, when cut open in the unripe stage, exudes a milky fluid. This fluid is allowed to dry, forming a sticky, brownish mass which is further dried and powdered. This powder is unrefined opium.

Heroin smuggled into the United States comes from two main areas, Mexico and the Near East, particularly Iran and Turkey. The actual manufacture or conversion of crude opium into heroin is carried on not only in these countries, but also in Western Europe, especially in France and Italy—possibly because these countries have long Mediterranean coastlines that make smuggling easy. Heroin also arrives in the United States from Southeast Asia, a route made easier in recent times by the heavy war-support traffic between the United States and such countries as Laos and Thailand.

The International Narcotics Control Board of the United Nations believes that in spite of intensive efforts to shut off these sources, little success has been achieved. It should be remembered that the livelihood of many thousands of families in the Middle East, Latin America, and Asia depends on the illicit opium market. Mexican officials reported that in 1969 they had discovered and destroyed 4,322 poppy plantations, and even allowing for exaggerated "poppy counts" one wonders what happens to those farmers and their families, already desperately poor, who are deprived in this way of income. It is certain that many countries, because of just such social and economic considerations, have been less than wholehearted in their efforts to halt or curtail production of opium and its refined product, heroin.

Heroin is most commonly referred to in this country by those who use it or deal in it as "smack," "horse," "junk," or "snort." It is usually sold in small cellophane or plastic bags known as "packs," "decks," or "bags." It is a grayish-white or brownish-white powder that is dissolved in water—usually by heating in a teaspoon—before injection into a vein (a practice called "mainlining"), usually an accessible vein in the forearm. Veins that have been jabbed with needles many times tend to close off and be replaced with fibrous or scar tissue, and infection from a contaminated needle will hasten this process. The linear scars in and beneath the skin of addicts are known as "tracks." Sometimes heroin is injected directly beneath the skin, a practice termed "skin-popping," but this method soon gives way to mainlining; later the mainlining addict might have "used up" all his easily accessible superficial veins and resort to skin-popping once more. (An Edinburgh physician, Dr. Alexander Wood, is credited with the invention of the hypodermic syringe in 1853. Ironically, his wife became addicted to morphine and was the first recorded victim of accidental death from the injection of opiates.)

Heroin can also be taken by "snorting"—literally that—snorting it up into the nasal passages where it is easily absorbed through the soft mucous membrane that makes up the inner lining of the nose and pharynx. A heroin addict is called a "junkie." To understand what being a junkie means, we must first describe the effects of heroin on the body and the mind.

The effects of heroin

Heroin has a remarkable capacity to diminish both physical and mental pain. These analgesic and sedative effects are achieved without excessive drowsiness. However, the drug does cause lethargy and apathy, a turning inwards without the redeeming quality of reflectiveness. There is also a numbing of sensibility not only to pain but also to the subtleties of human relationships. In a word, heroin is a depressant to the brain. The effect of the drug on physical pain is curious. There is no doubt that the threshold for the perception of pain is raised by the general depression of brain functions, so that a greater stimulus is needed to bring about the same degree of pain perception. At the same time, however, pain does continue to be "felt" but in a different way; it is as if heroin allows the user to detach himself from the pain and no longer concern himself with it. In this sense the pain remains but becomes more bearable. Heroin also relieves tension and anxiety and induces mild euphoria, or a sense of well being. This euphoria is more pronounced in those who are suffering in one way or another at the time they take heroin. In fact, if a "normal" person, neither addicted to the drug nor in physical or psychological pain, takes heroin, he can become depressed rather than euphoric. While the mood induced is usually satisfying and one of relief, there is at the same time a clouding of the intellect. If the user decides to sleep, he can do so easily and dreams are usually pleasant, but not always so.

When the heroin is mainlined, some of the sensations described are heightened and intensified. The user may experience real pleasure in the way he perceives his body, and many will say that the closest they can come to describing this experience in ordinary language is that it resembles a prolonged orgasm. Soon after taking heroin the addict may have an acute bout of nausea and vomiting—often referred to as a "good sick," because for some unknown reason the sought-after effects of heroin appear to be more pronounced if vomiting occurs, or so it is reported. His marked apathy, listlessness, and inertia prevent the addict from working productively and even interfere with his ability to take adequate care of his own bodily needs, so it is clear that it is extremely difficult for him to hold down a job.

After about four hours, the effects of heroin have more or less tapered off, and if the user is not addicted, if he is "experimenting" with the drug, he may have no more after-effects than slight irritability, if that. However, what anguish and pain the user might have been suffering before taking the drug will return as the drug's effects wear off. And here lies the danger. For those who live lives of intolerable pain and indignity, for those who see death as a blessed relief, the choice of heroin as an escape is one of the few choices left; and clearly many will make that choice in full knowledge of the dangers, in the conviction that life offers them nothing better.

If heroin is taken frequently, the body reacts by demanding a constant supply of the drug; and if this is not forthcoming, severe symptoms will follow. At this point addiction has been established, and the heroin addict knows that these symptoms can only be relieved by taking more heroin or a related opiate. Physiologically, the primary effects of heroin, except in the case of overdosage, are not life threatening. Respiration and heart rate are both diminished, blood pressure may drop moderately, and the pupils will become very small. Brain function in general is dampened down. Heroin and the other opiates also have a specific effect on the activity of the intestinal tract, and it is of course well known that paregoric, which contains morphine, is very helpful in quieting diarrhea, and that codeine, another alkaloid present in raw opium, frequently causes constipation.

Dangers of heroin

An overdose of heroin can kill, as we are learning all too frequently in the agonized reports that now come from the suburbs as well as from the inner cities. Some of the children now its victims are the children of parents who have voice and power in community affairs. No longer is heroin addiction felt to be exclusively a ghetto problem. Perhaps at last the deaths of children in the ghettoes from heroin will no longer be ignored. We can only hope so.

How does heroin kill? An overdose can cause deep sleep

or coma but the most dangerous effect is on the respiratory system. Breathing rate may be reduced to two or three times a minute, greatly decreasing the supply of oxygen to the body. Death can follow from oxygen starvation of the brain. The signs of acute heroin poisoning are deep sleep or coma, cold, clammy and sometimes bluish skin (from lack of oxygen), small, often pinpoint pupils. When the brain is severely deprived of oxygen, the pupils will open wide; this change from pinpoint pupils to wide open pupils is usually a sign of impending death. As mentioned, there is marked depression of respiration; at this stage, even if respiration is restored to normal, death can follow from complications such as pneumonia or edema (waterlogging) of the lungs. Blood pressure falls rapidly and the victim may go into shock, further diminishing the supply of oxygen to the vital centers of the brain.

The chance of an overdose is especially great, because the user has no way of knowing the exact strength of the dose he is taking (the pusher can vary the strength of the mixture according to what he thinks he can get away with); and the user therefore risks his life each time he injects the drug into his system. Furthermore, the material used to "cut" the heroin might in itself be dangerous, less likely from malice than from ignorance.

Continued use of heroin, even without overdose, can also cause serious illnesses—even death—as a consequence of the severe general debilitation and poor resistance to infection that are common concomitants of addiction to heroin.

Death can also result from the introduction of infection by the use of contaminated materials, syringes, or needles. A number of heroin addicts have developed severe infections of the valves of the heart that have proved fatal. Needless to say, this particular complication is not specific to heroin; any drug

83

that is injected in a similar way carries such danger. For the same reason, hepatitis from contaminated needles is a not unusual complication of heroin addiction.

Heroin, we repeat, is a dangerously addicting drug and if taken frequently, the body rapidly develops a tolerance to it, so that increasing doses must be taken to achieve the same effects. This tolerance levels off but not before large amounts —usually between 100 and 150 milligrams—are taken each day. The monetary cost of maintaining such an addiction is high; and because the addict is unable to work while on the drug, he may—and often does—take desperate steps to get the money to pay for the heroin.

If the person addicted to heroin wishes to stop taking the drug, he knows he must face up to withdrawal symptoms; these are greatly feared, although often exaggerated through such fears. He knows well enough the profound anxiety, irritability, and painful hypersensitivity to sound and light and touch he experiences if he does not get his "fix" in time. The actual intensity of withdrawal symptoms depends on the degree of addiction. Withdrawal can take the form of yawning, sweating, and mild irritability accompanied by sniffling and moist eyes—due to increased activity of moisture-producing cells in the eyes and nose. Far more severe symptoms will typically unfold if the person was taking large doses of heroin each day for several weeks and then stopped abruptly. Between twelve and sixteen hours after the last dose of heroin the mild symptoms just described begin to appear. These become steadily worse, with increasing restlessness, anxiety, a desire for sleep but an inability to sleep, uncomfortable "gooseflesh" feelings, and marked loss of appetite.

About twenty-four hours after the onset of symptoms or thirty-six hours after the last dose the addict develops muscle twitching and severe cramps in the abdomen, back, and legs. He perspires freely. He shakes. He feels cold. Vomiting and diarrhea compound his wretchedness. There is no doubt that the suffering can be excruciating, and as it does not quickly subside, one can understand why "going cold turkey" (abruptly stopping heroin intake without any substitute drug) is dreaded by addicts. Withdrawal symptoms reach greatest intensity between two and three days after the last dose and then subside slowly over the next one or two weeks. It is an exhausting and frightening experience and one that leaves the addict weak and depressed. During this period he usually loses a great deal of weight.

Thomas De Quincey wrote this of his experience withdrawing from opium:

> Meantime the symptoms which attended my case for the first six weeks of the experiment were these: enormous irritability and excitement of the whole system; the stomach, in particular . . . often in great pain; unceasing restlessness night and day; sleep—I scarcely knew what it was—three hours out of the twenty-four was the utmost I had, and that so agitated and shallow that I heard every sound that was near me; lower jaw constantly swelling; mouth ulcerated; and many other distressing symptoms that would be tedious to repeat, among which, however, I must mention one because it had never failed to accompany any attempt to renounce opium . . . sneezing. This now became exceedingly troublesome, sometimes lasting for two hours at once and recurring at least twice or three times a day.

We cannot emphasize too strongly that addiction to heroin can be established very rapidly. The person who takes one, two, or three bags of heroin always puts himself in some danger of getting "hooked" despite any assurance he may feel to the contrary. But we would do well to remember that the combination of ghetto, heroin, and hopelessness is a particularly lethal one. As for our suburban youth, they may be angry, bored, resentful, disaffected, "alienated," frustrated, and so on, yet our society gives them much more attention than it gives to children of the ghetto; and therefore their chances of surviving heroin addiction are, on the whole, that much greater.

Rather obviously no one can possibly know exactly how many people use marijuana, or with what frequency and devotion. The law forbids us in the United States to use the drug, and so all estimates of who does and how often must in the first place take into account the reluctance of people to admit an unlawful interest and, conversely, the sensational desire some have to admit just that.

According to many newspaper reports in recent years, over half the students in certain colleges take marijuana at least once, and a third use the drug repeatedly, if not with a frequency that amounts to regularity. Moreover, marijuana is being used by increasing numbers of children of secondary school age—and in junior high schools as well as high schools and private academies. Again, there is no way to be completely certain how accurate polls and questionnaires are, but deans, professors, head masters or principals, school physicians, lawyers, and district attorneys who have constant and immediate contact with youthful drug

87

users (only some of whom become, in turn, recorded as drug offenders) do in large measure agree; however "impressionistic" and variable their estimates may be, the consensus of these professional men is that more and more young people are trying marijuana. In late 1969 Weldon H. Smith, coordinator of narcotic programs for California's Department of Corrections informed New York State's Narcotic Addiction Control Commission that "experimentation with and chronic use of marijuana pervades almost every sector of our society that contains the age group of 14 to 30."*

Some reports and estimates may be inflated or may represent hysterical, panicky (or boastful) responses by self-conscious people—both old and young—who live in a contemporary atmosphere filled with rumor and hungry for evidence of melodrama and scandal. On the other hand, the issue of the incidence of marijuana use causes surprisingly little argument between advocates and opposers of the drug. Most observers agree that in the past decade marijuana has become increasingly used by middle-class suburban youths, both in schools and colleges, whereas a few decades ago the drug was largely unheard-of among such students. To be sure, one must ask which youths use pot in which suburbs of which sections of the country, and, for that matter, in which colleges and in which geographical region.

---

* "A conservative estimate of persons in the United States, both juvenile and adult, who have used marijuana at least once is about 8 million and may go as high as 12 million people. Can you imagine what would happen to the law enforcement and corrections systems of this country if each of these 12 million people had been caught by a policeman when smoking his first marijuana cigarette? It is time to change from a prosecution to a public health approach in dealing with drug abuse, and especially in cooling the marijuana problem. . . ."—Dr. Stanley Yolles, director of the National Institute of Mental Health, United States Public Health Service, in 1969 before the House Select Committee on Crime.

The suburbs of Columbia, South Carolina, or Sioux City, Iowa, or Helena, Montana are not those of Atlanta, Saint Louis, Los Angeles, New York City, Chicago, or San Francisco. Colleges such as Harvard, Berkeley, the University of Chicago, or the University of Michigan should not be confused with the many other private or state-supported schools whose students are significantly less inclined to activist politics, to the use of drugs, and to recently favored variations in clothing style and hair length. Yet, marijuana is by no means used only by upper-middle-class political liberals who live on the East and West Coasts and in certain isolated spots scattered across the nation. Many of the poor who live in our urban ghettoes use marijuana, among other drugs, as do an increasing number of so-called middle-to-lower-middle-class youths, some of whom have no interest in politics, our foreign policy, or racial problems.

Of considerable social significance is the pattern of drug use that has emerged: in the ghetto many youths use marijuana; and way across town, in the affluent suburbs, youths who are neither poor nor black also use marijuana, and in growing numbers. What is to be made of that? Are the rich falling prey to the vices of the poor? Have the nation's social and racial struggles somehow precipitated an alliance of sorts among young people of different backgrounds? Does the use of marijuana by various and seemingly incompatible groups represent one more example of the kinds of ironies America has always possessed? Such questions are very much tied to the fact that marijuana has a common appeal across class lines even as in certain rural areas the poor and the rich share a common *lack* of interest in drugs.

The interviews in this and following chapters, in which young men and women are asked why they take marijuana, illustrate how dangerous it is to generalize about the motives and circumstances of people who smoke pot. The interview below is with a young resident of a northern ghetto—a fourteen-year-old black youth who is, in fact, a very old and tired man:

I've been smoking so long I couldn't give you a figure on how long—five years, I'd say, more or less. I don't keep track. I don't count the times, the years. My cousin and his friends, they started us. They gave us the stuff. They taught us how. My cousin, he said to me: "George, you've got to know how to leave, man, you really do." I didn't know what he was meaning. I told him he was talking crazy. He said I could find out, if I wanted, if he was crazy or not. He gave me the cigarette and I took it in, the pot, and I liked it. I saw what he was saying. I got a little high, I must have. That was a long time ago. I don't remember that far back; I don't remember everything. All I know is this: you use the stuff, and you get real loose, and you're off on a cloud a little. You're gone. You've left. You see?

I like pot. It's good. You don't go *too* high. You're cool. It's good to use when you want to cool yourself down. My friends, all of them, use it sometimes. Some are fooling around with stronger stuff, but not me. I see too many people around here that are hooked. They're ruined. They're done, all washed up. I've taken other things. I've tried. I've experimented, you know. But I don't go for those big "highs," not like you hear people describe them. I'd like to have a lot of money and own a place in Nevada, in Las Vegas. I hear that's where you see money, lots of it, at the wheels, the machines. I take too much pot and I forget where I've put my coat; you get like that, you forget all over the place. You don't care. Maybe you shouldn't care. I do, though. I'm looking forward to driving, and I hope I'll one day have a big car. The people who drive big cars, they don't use a lot of drug stuff. They sell to others. You got to be smart. My old man knows the ropes around here. He says to let other people want to buy, and you be ready to sell what they want, and that's how to get money. He's right.

I've never used a needle; I wouldn't let a needle get near any vein of mine. I'd kill someone who tried to get me hooked. I like pot, but that's no needle game. Who the hell thinks pot will lead to the needle? That's up to you. If you're heading for the needle, you are. If you're not, they couldn't make you touch a needle even if *they* pay you—and there are pushers who will. They'll tell you: look, the first few times we'll give you the stuff free to try, and we'll give you some money, so you don't have to work, and you can relax and enjoy yourself. You know what I say? They can try someone else. I let them know. They know anyway, though. They know who's ready and who isn't. One pusher I know better than the others (he's my brother's friend) told me it takes him half a minute to figure who's going to get hooked and who isn't. He can read their minds and see what their minds say by the look in their eyes, he says.

What does smoking pot have to do with the needle? Whoever heard of turning from one to the other—unless you're going for the needle, you've got the hunger in you, and you're experimenting, you're fooling around, you're looking for something to take for the hunger. You'll never be happy until you're hooked. Then you stop smoking pot. If you're on the needle, you don't want pot. If you take pot and you're not satisfied, you go to the needle. If you take pot and it's what you want, you stay right there. I'm right here. I'm staying right here. No one's moving me. No one's going to push me. No one's moving my friends. No one's pushing them. We harvest the grass and burn it up and that's all we're after—except money, you know. The trouble is, there's not a lot of money around here—more grass and more needles than dollar bills, I believe that.

Literally ten miles away—ten very long miles—a fifteen-year-old youth also talks about marijuana. Although the two speakers are about the same age, both Americans, and almost neighbors—they live in the same state in adjoining cities—they don't talk alike:

I've tried pot. I don't use it all the time, just certain times. No one uses it all the time. That's a lot of crazy talk. We go to

91

someone's house and we turn on. What's so bad about that? We like to do it. You feel good. You're free. You don't lose your mind. You don't have a hangover. You just feel good—good and free. Is there anything wrong with feeling free? Anything bad? Why shouldn't a guy take in a few deep breaths, inhale some grass, then lean back and feel good? I don't see anything, no images or pictures or anything. I don't hear anything—nothing. All that happens is that I feel myself loosening up. My muscles relax; I feel good, that's all I can say. I feel free.

Sometimes I feel better than other times. Maybe it's the pot, how good it is. Maybe it's just me. I wouldn't take pot before an exam, or if I were going for an interview at a college. If I did, I might start asking myself *why*—why I memorize all the junk I do in school, and why everyone climbs all over everyone else to get ahead, always to get ahead. When you start thinking like that, you're in danger of dropping out. I don't want to drop out, but I have the right to stop sometimes and go slow. That's what smoking grass does for me—that's *all* it does, but that's a lot. I mean, it helps me cool down and look, really look; it slows the world down for you, so you can ask yourself and your friends what you're doing and what you're after. I told my father he ought to ask himself questions like that. You know what he said. It's predictable, it really is: "I haven't got time. You won't either when you're my age, and you've got a family to support and all the tuition bills of your kids."

I asked him why he wanted us all to go to fancy schools and colleges, and he said we're spoiled, asking questions like that. We should be glad we're there. I am. I don't argue with him on that score. He's right. But you can't be blind all the time—and work, work like him, my dad. I get good grades. I'm not on top, but I'm not on the bottom. I play a good game of squash. I'm on the baseball team. I make out; I make out pretty good. Most of my friends use pot; they smoke grass and so do I—not a lot, but sometimes, once a week or twice a month, it depends. If my father knew that, he'd think I was a criminal or something. I could tell him I'm doing fine in school and I was on the baseball team, but he wouldn't care. He says if you start with drugs, you end up in jail and you're finished for life. I hope

I never get like that. I hope I never get so old I'm completely out of it. I hope I keep my cool on things.

You can't talk to older people about drugs. In school they give you this story that "one thing leads to another"; that's all they tell you. And if they're not saying that, they hit you with your "problems"—your problems, your problems; that's all they talk about. ("You're going through a difficult time," and all that.) If that doesn't work, if you tell them there's nothing wrong with you, nothing troubling you, and you're not going to take heroin—tomorrow or any other day—they'll tell you that last thing: you can't violate the law. The law is the law—I've heard that about one million times, I'd say, conservatively speaking. They don't know how funny they sound when they get up and start preaching at you for turning on—once a week at the most. And if you tell them about liquor and cigarettes, the millions of alcoholics and the deaths caused by driving under the influence, and cancer of the lungs, they stiffen up—the teachers, the school doctor, and the psychologists they bring in here— and they say "two wrongs don't make a right," or "I'm not talking about alcohol or cigarettes, but drugs."

No one has dared tell them to their face that turning on with grass on Friday night with your friends is not becoming a *drug addict*. God, they love to call you that, a *drug addict*. They seem to think they can scare you or something. *They're* scared; or they just don't know how it is. They've never smoked grass, and they talk as if we're going to end up criminals, you know, or in a mental hospital or something.

So it goes in the ghetto and in the well-to-do suburbs. It is, of course, easy to dismiss the claims of these two youths, to dismiss them as partisan, brash, thoughtless, or exaggerated. On the contrary their remarks (edited slightly) exemplify how youths talk today and what they have to say. By no means are their words, thoughts, and strong opinions unrepresentative— or without moments of intelligence, shrewdness, and a kind of astringent common sense, which many older people like to dismiss as immaturity or worse. For the ghetto youth marijuana is familiar and pleasant; for the suburban youth marijuana is also pleasant, but the cause of endless arguments, discussions, accusations, and refutations.

Other comparisons emerge, as the words of these two youths are examined. For instance, in neither youth has the use of marijuana really thwarted ambition (although the money and influence one youth wants, the other can clearly take for granted and perhaps consider throwing aside). And neither young man expresses any intention of going on to harder drugs.

A cigarette or pipe does not necessarily lead to a syringe. Still, many in the ghetto, who begin with marijuana and then try heroin, in a short time become addicts; and the same progression from marijuana to heroin takes place among suburban youths. But which youths are able to try pot, use it, and enjoy it, without hunting down any and every other drug until the drug experience becomes life's entire purpose? On the other hand, which youths start with pot, then leave it in a wild rush for a *better* drug—stronger and more consuming?

The ghetto youth just quoted has an answer that may be as good as any. He says that he and others like him are hungry, perhaps literally hungry for food and certainly hungry psychologically in ways that millions of words would be too few to describe: hungry for escape; hungry for the fog or the clouds; hungry for a star up in the sky that, though cold, barren, and deserted, offers sanctuary—a haven of sorts, a place of rest and quiet, a home from which other people (indeed the rest of the universe) could be watched and appreciated and often enough scorned.

That young man of fourteen, prompted a little, expands on the word *hunger,* and in so doing speaks not only about his own people—his own friends and neighbors, crowded into the broken-down tenements of a particularly bleak and dreary northern ghetto—but says something too about other young people who share with him little but a generation's time:

Sure, they're hungry, that's what. A man who shoots horse [takes heroin] is hungry. You can't feed him, either. He's hungry for something that nobody's got. That's what my brother says. That's what I say. You ever talk with them, man? You ever hear them when they're high? I don't mean when they're in a *hospital*, coming down; hell, no—then they'll have a different line, being there in a hospital, and with the doctors around and their buddies, their lover-boys, the cops. I mean here, when they're way, way up. They smile, man. It's the only time they smile. One of them, he tells me he never can smile to save himself except when he's shooting, and he's got it in him, and then he gets loose, real loose. He feels warm inside and quietlike. He says he wants to smile, and he sees everyone else smiling and happy, real happy. He's wrong, you know. But that's his business; if he thinks the world is smiling at him, that's his right to go and believe himself. I don't want to argue him down. Why should I? If a man can find himself a little peace for a while, then good luck to him; but a guy like me, I know better. I'll have people smiling at me one day, if I have enough money. With money, you can keep smiling longer than if you use the needles.

My brother and my cousin say you can have a million dollars and you could still be feeling bad. Right! They're right! You can have zero dollars and feel bad, too. I'd rather feel bad and have a million dollars. Then, if I was so bad and down that I started using the needles, I'd be able to hire me a lawyer. He could run interference for me. He could call the shots. He could pay people off. Everyone would listen to me, even if my arms were all marked up, from my wrists all the way to my shoulders. But, man, you don't go hitting your veins just because you're in bad shape one day. I feel lousy sometimes. I feel as bad as a guy can feel. So, what I do is try to eat something I like. I play pool. I smoke grass. I wait for my number to come up. I don't hit my veins. I don't go cutting into my skin, no sir, I don't.

95

Drugs and Youth

A guy who's got money, and he tells you he's going to do that—use the needle—he's something else. He's not picking up those needles just because he's smoked himself some grass. You go and ask the guys on horse; they'll tell you they're hungry, that's why they're on horse, and they were ready for the needle before they ever smoked grass or anything else. They knew it fitted them—horse. That's what I've heard them say. They say it's right for them, just right. Hell, grass is nothing for them— nothing, a big nuisance, a big nothing, a crumb of bread, a laugh. They'll tell you if you go and ask them.

He has a point, and more than a minor one. The essence of his observations could be dressed up in all sorts of pretentious, self-important phrases, yet tell no more than what he has simply said: that addiction to heroin, to hard drugs, is not just a matter of trying marijuana and then inevitably progressing to other drugs, to addiction, and to the needle. If there is such a thing as an "addictive personality," the causes are complicated and by no means tied to a particular person's experience with marijuana or, for that matter, any other single drug.

The "hunger" that shrewd young man describes, which is found in prosperous neighborhoods as well as ghettoes, can set in motion any one of dozens of harmful, even dangerous "addictions," or compulsions. There is no evidence that marijuana is an addictive drug; nor is there any conclusive evidence that the use of marijuana *in and of itself* leads to cocaine or heroin addiction.

Some individuals (it is not known how many) use marijuana, enjoy it, and never take an interest in other drugs. Some individuals (it is not known how many) take marijuana and soon go on to cocaine, heroin, LSD, speed, or whatever. Some individuals (it is not known how many) start out with morphine or heroin and never try anything else but them, the

96

hardest of the so-called hard drugs. If all these statements are true, then what is to be concluded—about marijuana's role, so to speak, in the problem of drug addiction and about the use the drug is put to, whether in the ghetto or the suburbs? One of the most vexing aspects of the entire marijuana problem is this: we do not know in a thoroughly clear-cut way whether marijuana, in pure and moderate doses, can indeed be taken over a long period of time safely, enjoyably, casually, occasionally, and voluntarily rather than compulsively. Because the drug is illegal, we are unlikely to know about the many who for years go about their everyday business and at times smoke marijuana, with no evidence of harmful consequences.

In drawing conclusions, the importance of a rational, thoughtful analysis—one that shuns panic, sweeping accusations, and sweeping generalizations—arises again. It would be satisfying to jumble everything up and come out with a few sharp, handy, easy "answers," but the drug scene won't lend itself to clear-cut, unambiguous rules, solutions, or even explanations.

Both youths previously quoted seem to comprehend what many people are unwilling even to take note of: that it is not wise to look at an essentially emotional matter through thoroughly tidy and logical eyes. In other words, *it all depends*— it all depends on who takes how much marijuana and why; it all depends on where the drug is being used and whether the user is alone or in company; and, if with others, which others, and intent upon what purposes.

Everyone agrees that marijuana in moderate or "ordinary" amounts is not an addictive drug and is not poisonous, lethal, or severely toxic. The use of pot doesn't (so far as we now know) damage brain tissue, bring injury to the body's nerves or any of

97

its vital organs, or cause cancer or heart disease. The use of pot does bring about psychological reactions, some of them rather uncertain and variable at that. Against such a background one can only raise questions—not futile and vague, but necessary and clarifying questions, questions that must be asked, in the clear expectation that answers will not be simple and clear-cut, but rather complex.

Why, for example, do some ghetto youths shun drugs altogether, while others accept marijuana and use it moderately, while still others take any and every drug around to secure oblivion (and too often a quick end to their short and brutish lives)? Furthermore, why do some suburban youths seek drugs—all sorts of drugs—while others demonstrate no such interest?

Do the answers lie in changing social customs? Is there some psychological craving, need, or problem that prompts a youth to smoke pot or cigarettes, to swallow dexedrines or liquor, to take things that stimulate the body or slow it down, that prod the mind or put it to rest? Can words like *history* and *culture* lead us to understand why at a given time a large number of people from a particular section of this planet become interested in tobacco or marijuana or conversely lose such an interest?

More precisely, as the year 2000 approaches, are we in the United States perhaps seeing an erosion of what Max Weber called "the protestant ethic and the spirit of capitalism"? That is, are we getting more and more caught up in values vastly different from the ones once upheld as right and true—values even then, in the good old days, hard to follow completely, or sometimes at all? For all the glibness of the phrase, is a "youth culture" growing in America, growing significantly in real life rather than only in the minds of social scientists or self-styled social critics in pursuit of something to write about? Is it by the authority of a growing "youth culture" that marijuana becomes far more acceptable to so many reasonably sane and sensible young people?

Is it not true that East is going West, and vice versa, in the sense that habits, beliefs, and attitudes now cross continents instantaneously? Is it not difficult for anyone, anywhere —least of all America's curious, prosperous middle-class youth —to live apart, to fall back contentedly on his heritage?

Does an industrial society reach a certain point of development, achievement, and productivity, then begin to slow down and change its direction of thrust? Don't comfort and leisure gradually affect more and more people, making them less hard-working, less driving, less austere, less assertively busy and meticulous, less restrained, and less dedicated to the future rather than the present? For that matter, ought not the question be phrased rather more affirmatively? Has a time come when, at last, many of our youth desire more meditative, introspective lives—lives in which they serenely share rather than earnestly seek after, in which they reach out to others rather than carve out for themselves *their* world, *their* domain?

Since we hope to deal pointedly and modestly with the medical, psychiatric, and legal aspects of drug use (rather than with large-scale economic, political, religious, and philosophical changes), this book cannot do proper justice to the questions above, though it cannot ignore such matters, either. Time and time again young people ask similar questions, and not always in a fashion that can be reassuringly dismissed as muddled, half-baked, or superficial. In fact, perhaps the "experts" should be asked for answers to the questions of young people—not altogether unlike theirs, if more forcefully and perhaps embarrassingly worded. For example, the following remarks perhaps ring a familiar note to many a teacher, parent, or youth, yet are rather easy for some experts to ignore when they set out to ask the whys of marijuana use:

You want to know answers. You ask questions, and we're supposed to give you reasons. That's the whole point; when we smoke grass we drop that whole bag. That's not our scene anymore—the quiz, the good answers, the wrong answers, or maybe "half-credit." That's what the French teacher keeps on saying: "guess you lose a credit," or "guess you gain a credit," or "half-credit." I've smoked before his class, just a few drags. Nothing really happens to me when I take pot, to answer your question. I mean, I think a little more, that happens. During his class I thought a little more when I went to it a little stoned. I decided to go in and watch what happens—you know, as if I was making a film. I've never learned so much; maybe not French, but about him, the teacher, and about us—how we act, you know, in a room like that. He called on my friends—two of them—and I thought I was seeing them for the first time. They wanted to give the right answer, but they were laughing inside at the way he carries on, that poor teacher. He means well, but is he gone, really lost! I'd see my friend trying, trying so hard you could cry looking at him, and yet you could see, you could see he didn't give a damn. (I asked him afterwards, and he said what we all say: it's a game—you have to get the marks to stay in school, to go to college, to get a good job, to live well, and on, and on, and on.)

The worst thing to see was that teacher, though—especially when he got a little mixed up himself and didn't know what to do. For him everything is "credits"; those credits of his! He should have been an accountant; gains and losses—that's all he keeps track of, that's all the other teachers keep track of, too. Will I give him an *A*— or a *B+*? Does he deserve a *B* or a *B*—? Should he get *85* on this test, or only *80*? Should I recommend him, or recommend him highly, or *very* highly? Should he go to a state college, or the Ivy League, or the little Ivy League? You go to this school four years, and you hear stuff like that until you wonder who's crazy and who's in his right mind, and who to listen to and who to tell "go can it; go sell it someplace else."

I meant to tell you about the French teacher, though. He's not such a bad guy. He's a good guy, actually. He lives for teaching; you can see it. He doesn't ask himself what it's all about. Once a kid asked him if de Gaulle wasn't ruining Europe and too old to be up there as head—something like that—and the teacher, he didn't know what to say. Finally, he said we were studying French—the language, not the news you read in the papers. Anyway, if it hadn't been for the grass, I don't think I'd have caught him. That's what I did; like with a butterfly, when you get a net over it—or a good picture a photographer takes. The moment of truth, you could call it—when he called on my friend and he gave him part of the answer, but not all of it. The teacher sat there, and he didn't say anything for a few seconds. Usually he speaks right out: "credit" or "no credit." Instead, he waited. Then he said, "half-credit," then he waited. Then he said, "I guess."

It wasn't so much what he said, or even the way he took his time, but the look that came over his face. The poor guy was in pain. He didn't know what to do. Suddenly he burst out with a little sermon for us. He told us he'd keep on giving us those half-credits, like he has before, but "in life"—that's what he always says—"in life, in real life, you either win or lose; you get what you're after, or you don't."

I've heard it, all that, a million times—from my parents and other teachers and him, that French teacher, too. It's just that with a little grass in me I could see the whole picture: that teacher, trying to be fair, but feeling the outside world (that "real life" he talks about) breathing down on him; and his credits and no-credits, like I say, as if he was running a bank or something; and the worst of it, how he couldn't even live up to his own words. He's always telling us that the French really know how to enjoy themselves, and they're so smart and warm and pleasant to be with. He's always telling us that they know the score, and they're a real honest people. But he couldn't just admit that you can't split things into credit or no credit. I mean, he tried to, with the "half-credit," but he started sweating it, he started worrying.

The French aren't like that—if you believe what he says. They probably *are* like that, actually; a lot of them are. They're probably like us. That's what I'm trying to tell you: just because that teacher and my parents and my friends' parents and half of France and the United States think like that, doesn't mean *I* have to, or my buddies have to. We can sit around and turn on, and we don't go knocking down everyone, the way you hear we do. We don't. We sit and talk. We zero in on the truth—the important things—the best we can, the nearest we can get to it. We like it, like the feeling; inside you feel quiet, sort of, you do. It's hard to explain if you haven't tried it—just like if you're someone who really enjoys a cigarette, a regular cigarette, you can't explain why you like it, what you get out of it, to the next guy, who's never smoked a cigarette in his life.

I'm not trying to build this thing up; when we smoke grass, one guy might say nothing, not a thing is happening, and the next guy might really be turned on. By "turned on" I mean awake and thinking—noticing what really counts and forgetting what doesn't. I recall saying to myself in the French class that if only he could get turned on—the teacher; if only he could stop handing out all those credits of his, and pretending, fooling himself, you know. Maybe he'll never take to pot. Maybe a guy like that is too old to smoke grass, but he could at least have a glass of wine, French wine, and ask himself why—why he's always adding and subtracting. That's the man's way, I tell you, like a machine: you gain, you lose; you win, you're beaten; you'll get into college, you won't; you'll make it, you'll fall flat on your face.

Once he told us the French could have even been a greater country, but they didn't know how to pull together and keep their minds on the goals ahead. They debated and debated; they fought and argued and became too philosophical or something. They're moody, he said, and you waste time and energy that way. You hesitate, and that's not good. The times I told you, when I had some grass in my head, I saw him—and that's what was happening to him: he was hesitating, the poor guy. I sat there and I thought to myself that he must be trying to tell himself that it didn't matter if the kid got a credit or lost one, because what counted was what he was trying to say, and what we could hear him say, and hear the teacher say. But he couldn't let that kind of idea stick around too long, not and be a teacher in our school. So he hesitated, like the French, and hedged his bets, and then he felt so bad that he had to go and give us all that "real world" stuff. Every time we hear that—things like that—we know they're hung-up, the teachers are. Instead of asking questions, they're dishing out answers.

That's what I like about grass. It gets you thinking and wondering. We sit around for an hour or two, and we've really been sweating—real good sweat, like in tennis, not the kind where you're taking one of those stupid multiple-choice tests or trying to get a "credit" for yourself on a Friday afternoon, so you can tell your old man on the weekend, when he has ten minutes to spare for a quickie talk, that "yes," you're doing okay in everything, "including French."

And from a ghetto, another youth does not quite echo such interest and concerns, but doesn't quite dissociate himself from them either. He, too, knows what it is to confront circumstances that are, to say the least, wryly confusing:

If I smoked all the time, if I was using grass morning, noon, and night—well, man, this would be too much. I mean, I'd be laughing to myself all the time. The other day a cop came over and he wanted to know what we were doing. We said we were doing nothing. He said we could come up with better than that. We said okay, we were sitting around and having a real smooth time; we were having a platter party. He said he liked the music, but were we fooling around with the drugs. I said no, but was he getting himself high on too much beer and maybe a jigger of scotch. (I know him from a long time back.) He said he got my point, but if we take drugs we'll end up in jail, but if he goes and has a beer and a shot of whiskey, he'll be okay with the law. Then I told him that's what we were doing, right then, playing the platters and thinking to ourselves: now isn't there a better

103

way to do things in this country? He laughed and said we won that round; with that question we did.

So, there are many questions to answer—those asked by young men and women, those asked by their parents, and those posed somewhat rhetorically by authors of a book like this, which hopes to examine the question of drugs—what they "mean" and what they "do," inside the body and outside in homes, schools, and courthouses of this society. An important question—a thoroughly ambitious and impossible one in the context of a book this size; a preposterous question already asked too often in a century plagued at times by psychological soothsayers of various names and descriptions—becomes obvious: What does it mean to be young? What does it mean to be young and to ask questions as never before—to everyone's annoyance, maybe bewilderment, maybe utter resentment?

It is all too tempting for psychiatrists and lawyers to ignore that question and instead throw names at youths, like the ones quoted, who smoke marijuana: they are sick; they are disturbed; they have serious problems; they are in turmoil or mental disarray; and they are delinquents or lawless troublemakers, potentially or already so. Many youths who advocate marijuana deserve a few such categorical labels, but many do not.

It doesn't make much sense to try to pigeonhole, psychiatrically, most high school or college students who have tried grass, at least not *only* on that account and not at that particular time in their lives. The time of youth has a very special meaning—a meaning that adults, however good their intentions and broad their understanding, often simply fail to comprehend. Perhaps this lack of empathy stems not from ignorance or malice, but from forgetfulness. Adults forget what it was like "back then"; what they themselves thought and felt; what they looked for, went through, sought after, delved into, kicked around in their minds, put to others, demanded of them and of themselves, too.

Granted, America's youth have not lacked for analysis. This book does not purport to include a comprehensive study of how boys and girls grow up to become youths in America's small towns, stretched out as they are, or its ghettoes, filled up as they are becoming. But neither can it ignore or gloss over the *rightness* that many youths feel about taking drugs—the connection they draw between the time of life they know to be theirs and the drugs they call upon.

So, we move from youths who for one reason or another use drugs to the more general subject of youth—and do so in the hope that the young men and women we have just mentioned and others both like and unlike them are thought about as more, much more, than "drug-users" or "pot-heads" or wayward lawbreakers.

| Growing up

The use of marijuana by so many American youths is not evidence, pure and simple, of widespread incipient "sickness," mental illness, or psychopathology. Young men and women have enough trouble understanding themselves and being understood by others; the last thing they need is to be discredited in the language of contemporary psychiatric and psychoanalytic theory, which only serves as a thinly disguised substitute for older, less convincing, or merely less modish pieties.

Since everyone has his problems—no one is completely without worries or fears—it is not enough to explain that a youth smokes grass *because* he feels anxiety and wants to subdue it or *because* he feels afraid and wants to feel less so. Many youths who shun drugs, no doubt, likewise feel anxious, lonely, and afraid. No one lacks his moments of doubts—his irrational misgivings and times of unnecessary hesitation or suspicion. Indeed, it is somewhat naive to use terms such as *healthy* and *sick* to praise and condemn various forms of social behavior.

107

Although compassion may be the expressed motive, condescension, at the very least, is often the outcome.

We hope to spare both ourselves and the reader that condescending approach, that line of reasoning. We do believe that drugs, from marijuana to heroin, have definite psychological consequences for the user, and in the next chapter we spell them out, insofar as they are known. But first we want not only to talk about youth without making the discussion an exercise in pathology but also to make clear our conviction that for a good number of youths—not all, but certainly many—the use of marijuana has to do with growing up rather than going awry.

We will not shirk the obvious dangers of drugs. But hopefully neither will we clothe our discussion in the tone of impeccable authority and respectability, while youths are turned into caricatures of themselves: mere children, callow youngsters on the road to ruin, products of disturbed homes, or students hopelessly sidetracked.

Rather, we hope to take youthful grass smokers at their word, listen to them, and comply with their most frequent request—to "come across" or "level" with them. Rather than always to listen to our various formulations about their makeup, their ways, and their values, they want to hear honest responses to their own formulations. The obviously disturbed youth, who emotionally is on shaky ground, clearly needs whatever help he or she can find. Far more puzzling and vexing is the youth who does not seem troubled, yet smokes grass. *Are* we automatically to call him "ill," even though psychiatrists have long said that, almost by definition, adolescence is characterized by turmoil and tension?

"I use pot, I do," a youth says, and by no means is he

"sick" or confused. He is seventeen, enrolled in a good college —a tall, thin, blondish young man who is a first-rate skier and an excellent student, as he has been for years. He favors history and political science, thinks he might want to be a lawyer, plays squash and tennis when he cannot ski, follows the news closely, goes occasionally but not regularly to church— and he uses pot. Moreover, he has told his parents that he uses pot; their initial shock, fear, and strong disapproval have yielded somewhat, though they shudder at the undeniable possibility that their son might one day be arrested for possessing marijuana.

The world of less fortunate youths—with their dilemmas and the implications to be drawn from their experiences—is presented later, but honest inquiry cannot reserve concern only for the hurt, the dazed, the badly upset, the up-tight, and the hung-up. Here, drawn from several interviews are some of the young man's thoughts, edited only as necessary for his protection:

I hope that if you use my ideas, you let me speak for myself. I'm sick and tired of hearing all these experts—the world is full of them—speaking for me and my friends and telling people what we think, and what's going on in our heads, and why we do this, and think this, and believe in what we believe in. They make a living that way, I know. But have you read what they say? I read it, and I can't believe it's me, or my roommates, or my friends. We all laugh at it—at what we read. But you can't stop there, because you know that when you go home your parents will be right there, wanting to know if you're "in trouble" (that's what my mother is afraid of; that's what she keeps asking) and, if so, whether you'd "think of going to a doctor."

I say to her that she means psychiatrist, and she nods her head. She's not so sure I should go; she can't really see any evidence that I'm "in trouble." But since I told her and dad that

Drugs and Youth

I smoke sometimes—that I smoke grass—they've both been watching me—not my every move (they can't, I'm away from home) but discreetly, as discreetly as they can, anyway.

I'm amused at some of the things I hear them say, my parents; I also get angry at them. They tell me I could become an addict. They tell me I'll become "apathetic"—if I hear that word one more time! I'm bored with their fears, and I think they are, too. In fact, I don't believe they have any real reason to be afraid, except for one thing—that the police could raid our room. But they would have to arrest half of us—half the students in the college and plenty of younger teachers, too. I told my father that. I said he was exaggerating things.

I get pot from a friend, and he gets it from his cousin in New York. His cousin is no pusher; he's no criminal. Do you know how *he* gets it? He has a brother in Los Angeles, and the brother sends it to him—yes, by mail! The brother is a medical student; that's right. My roommate's brother is also a medical student, right here. He's used pot, on and off, since he was a junior in college. He likes it. He says that after an exam he and his friends smoke a little grass and unwind. A few weeks ago they were told by an older doctor that he's tried pot—that he doesn't like it as much as scotch, but that the laws are crazy, really crazy.

I don't like the laws, but just as bad as the laws are the "experts"—the doctors, the psychiatrists who keep on saying you have to be disturbed, or else you won't want to take pot, and you get sicker and sicker the more you use it: you lose your drive, and you start thinking magiclike, or something like that. Who do they see? They see people who get hung-up and go to talk with them. All of my friends say they wish those "shrinks" would stop talking about everyone, and speak about what they know—their patients. I don't have anything against them: they're doctors, and they're doing the best they can to help people. I once thought I might want to be one, a doctor—a surgeon, maybe.

It's foolish, though, the way some of them come on. They don't know how they're laughed at. They talk about all the

110

"effects" of marijuana. We read what they say. We go to hear them; and it's ridiculous, what they say, how they come on. You can tell they've never smoked. You can tell that *they're* the ones who are hung-up. They're not just giving advice; they are *against* something, and they're out to convert you and wipe out sin! They preach and preach; underneath that's what they do. They start with all the medical dangers and the psychiatric ones, and before they're through you start pinching yourself to find out if it's you—*you* they've been describing with all those words: *anxiety* and *phobias* and *addiction* and *adolescent behavior* and all the rest. They make us seem almost crazy to begin with, and all we need is a little pot, and that does it.

I don't go for the argument that pot is safer than alcohol or cigarettes. I don't go for the argument that pot makes you a better person—that you become more creative, and nicer, and all of that. I don't smoke because I'm unhappy with myself. I've been allowed to drink since I was sixteen or so, I'd guess. I could try sherry when I was small, a kid. I started drinking a couple of years ago because I liked the feeling; my parents do all the time, and my brother does, and we all relax. I take pot for the same reason. My friends use it. My girl friend does. The guy who teaches us sociology does, the guy who teaches the writing course does, and the graduate student who works with us in the chemistry lab does. Now are *they* all mixed-up teenagers? God, we're sick of those doctors leaning over and trying to be so cool and reasonable and understanding, and talking about adolescents, adolescents, adolescents. They don't know how they sound to us —us adolescents: preachy, oh so worried, and, most of all, full of themselves and their moralisms that come out, one after the other.

They've got a beautiful system, too; if you criticize them, you've got a problem. I'm taking a course in "dynamic psychology." If you say they're wrong, you're "blocking" on something. If you tell them to go shove it, you're "aggressive" and "defensive." We pay them more respect than they do us. We go and read their books; naturally we do—we're "curious" like they say an "adolescent" should be. I wish *they* were a little more curious. I wish they came over and said: "Look, we don't know a lot,

111

and especially when you talk about marijuana. We have never tried it, and like we say, there's a lot to learn about what it does."

They want to have it both ways, though. They want to say: "We don't know a lot, so the drug shouldn't be made legally available." *But* they then go on to say all they *do* know—how dangerous and debilitating it is; how it drives you mad; leads you into heroin and other hard drugs; ruins your whole life, to hear them talk. They've made up their minds; you can feel it when they talk. And they say things that show they don't stop and look at what's really going on. I mean, societies don't act only on the basis of laboratory experiments; if they did, tobacco and alcohol would be illegal.

The doctors keep on saying that there is a toxic chemical or something in marijuana, and that if you take it in high doses you can go crazy—people have had hallucinations and all that. You can take anything in high doses and get into trouble. The point is that hundreds and hundreds of thousands of us smoke grass maybe once or twice a week, sometimes once or twice a month; and we don't go crazy, and we don't get poisoned, and we're still working and studying and all the rest. No psychiatrist sees us. No doctor sees us. I've never told any dean about all this. I have friends—six or eight good friends—who are like me; they smoke the way I do and live the way I do.

We're not hippies. We're not dropouts. We've never been in trouble with the law. We're not tied up with crime. We're not headed for heroin and all that. Not a single one of us has been "shrinked"—not one. There must be thousands like us. Who's going to get up and tell the public about *that*—how it's possible to smoke grass sometimes, and enjoy it, and keep on living a "normal life"? Who's to decide what *that* is, anyway? I don't see how you can use the word *normal* without reminding yourself that in 1900 a guy with a beard is the pillar of the community—a general or a president of the United States—and now he's looked upon by pillars of the community as a hippie or God knows what.

When you talk about "normal" you're not talking about scientific judgments, but social ones, made by societies that go

112

through changes from century to century. That's pretty obvious to me—maybe because I'm a college student who's taken a few courses in history, and sociology, and things like that. It's not so obvious to the police, though—and the doctors, because a lot of doctors make a lot of statements about a lot of people they never have seen and never will see. It's too bad; it's too bad the doctors get themselves into that kind of "scene." They become ministers, preachers. And it's too bad the public never hears about us—the people who never go to hospitals and clinics and don't have hang-ups that a little grass won't get rid of, *or* a movie, or skiing. (Skiing is the best thing of all for a hang-up!)

Yes, this young man is sarcastic at times—"hostile" and "defensive" many psychiatrists might say with justification. As for his insistence that doctors by definition know a lot about diseased patients, but less about healthy and untroubled people, a growing number of physicians, psychiatrists, and psychoanalysts recognize how careful in that regard clinicians must be. The young man is right when he says that psychiatrists meet up with those who have stumbled and somehow lost a degree of balance, even as lawyers see for the most part those who have collided with the law. Nevertheless, doctors (and lawyers and authors and just plain parents) are not without a view of ordinary, reasonably sound and sturdy youths and their growth in mind, body, and spirit. There are indeed certain things about growing up, about being full-grown but still rather young, that have a distinct bearing on what can loosely be called "the drug problem."

Here, for instance, is another youth telling about himself, his concerns, and his struggles. He is not in the slightest interested in taking marijuana or any other drug—quite the contrary:

I'm young, I guess, but at times I feel old, real old—a lot older than my nineteen years, I'll tell you that. I wonder whether I'll live as long as my parents and become one myself—a parent.

113

I don't mean to sound so damn gloomy. It's just that one of my friends in school got killed in Vietnam, and another friend almost died in an auto accident, and both things happened a few months ago. You start thinking about all the troubles this world has—the wars and murders and assassinations—and you begin to wonder if we'll make it for very much longer on this earth, what with hydrogen bombs and missiles and all the rest.

I'd like to be a teacher, maybe. I'd like to teach in a high school; history is my field. Sometimes I think I should go to law school. My father is a lawyer. He's not so very happy with his work. He admits it to me. He's in a big firm; tax law is his field. He works for the big corporations, and I guess he saves them some money. He goes all over the country, from one company to another, talking with their presidents and vice-presidents and treasurers and all the rest of them that run a company. They tell him their problems, and he tells them not to worry, because he'll fix things up so they won't lose half the money they think they will. He's a genius with numbers, and he can read those tax laws and figure out the loopholes—the legal ones. He's smart and fast, and they like him, business men do. That's what my mother says. "Your father knows how to smile and get people to relax," she says, but then she adds the hooker, "The only person he doesn't get to relax is himself."

I'm supposed to take after my father, but I don't think I do. I look like him, but my values are different. He's a real pusher. He's always in there working, thinking up the angles. He admits it. He makes a lot of money and he gives us all we need, but he never stops and asks himself things. He doesn't wonder what it's all about. I've asked him that sometimes, and it's not that he's dumb or an arrogant Wall Street type, who calls you kooky just because you want to do a little thinking, a little *questioning*. No, he'll go for a walk with you and tell you that he's the way he is, and you're different. "I'm a scratcher, that's what I am, son." He'll talk like that. "I come from poor people and I had to work my way through college and law school. I had no time to do anything, to ask any questions—I just worked." I've never known what I'm supposed to say when he talks like that. He's not trying to be mean, but he looks at me and he wants me to understand all he's gone through in his life. Then, when I try to tell him what I'm going through, right now, he can't understand. I've even written him letters about how I feel, because I figured that way I'd make myself clearer; and he'd have time to read over my words a few times, so he would maybe see what I'm trying to say. But it never works. We just can't get across to each other, it seems. I took a course in psychology last year, and the teacher said that was how it goes sometimes. But I knew that before I heard him say it, or read it in any book.

A lot of time I feel like those Greek philosophers must have felt. I mean I'm looking at people and I feel I'm up on a mountain, far away. I'm not crazy, I know. I'm doing fine. It's just that I don't always feel in the best shape. I don't feel like pushing, pushing, like my dad does. I want to sit back and read and lie in the sun, or I want to go swimming, that's all—not worry about what I have to do, and where I'm going after college, and what I want to be. It's pretty sad, I'll tell you, thinking about the rat race people get themselves into and call it "happiness."

I once asked my parents if they were happy, and, you know what, they both got so nervous I thought they'd go and collapse on me. They wigged out. They really did. My dad finally mumbled something about not having the time to think of things like that, and my mother said ditto for her; she was too busy keeping the house going, and all that—the activities she has. Then I told them I thought life meant more than that. I told them what *they* used to tell me—what the minister keeps on telling us, all of us, on Sundays. My father listened. He tried to, but the phone rang, and he was glad—*was* he glad!—to get out. He ran out. He said he'd take it on the other phone, when he was sitting right next to a phone. And he didn't come back, not for an hour. He had "some paper work," he told me later. And my mother—she had to go shopping, suddenly she did. She must have looked hard for something to buy and bring home. She came back with cooking apples and made an apple pie. We already had cooking apples, I noticed, but the pie was good, as usual. I guess that's her definition of what "happiness" is—eating apple pie. If she'd only say so, I actually wouldn't mind.

But in one breath she'll tell me all the old clichés about doing good, and being good, and "being of service to others"—the Red Cross, the hospital fund—and in the next, she's telling me and my sister how we've got to stick up for ourselves, since no one else will, and how you only get what you deserve, and you only deserve what you've fought for and won for yourself, and that's the way she expresses herself. Then I'll ask her about happiness —happiness, Mother!—and she says you shouldn't get yourself tied up with that kind of "notion." You know why? Because "you'll get slowed down," that's what she says. I asked her why I shouldn't stop and think over where I'm going, and she said there's too much to do in this world and that dreamers never get things done.

I'm not a dreamer, but I do wonder about a lot of things; and I'm not going to stop wondering, I hope. It's a strange thing, what happens to parents. They tell you all the right things to do when you're little. Then when you get older, they expect you to forget—forget a whole lot of what they've said, because you've got to be practical, they say. Maybe so; maybe you've got to be practical. But I sure hope I don't fall asleep like my dad has, stop thinking like he has. He admits it to me: "I haven't the time, the way you do." I'd like to make my life different, so that I *do* have the time.

This young man has more, much more, to think and, in his own word, *wonder* about. What kind of girl does he want to marry? Where should they live? What about the war, the draft, and the American political scene? Yet, throughout his remarks run certain themes, whatever the subject he is discussing. He feels in-between—not quite grown up, not a child, but not a husband and father either. As a result, he is time-conscious and not quite sure of himself, hence vulnerable, a bit gloomy, and a bit too worried about life's brief length, about death, and destruction. He is not quite ready to "adjust" —to make his compromises with the middle-class American world to which he was born and in which he will doubtless live all his life. He feels rebellious and uneasy with his parents; he is suspicious of them and particularly sensitive to their hypocrisies, weak spots, blind spots, duplicities, evasions, and compromises. He is not however *only* disenchanted with his parents; he also loves them and respects them and most certainly wants to draw near them, engage them in discussions as well as argument. But somehow the discussions don't work. His idealism embarrasses his parents, who hear their old words and phrases preached back at them with startling vigor and clarity. They hear what to them can only mean a lot of chatter, ironically made possible by, of all things, their social and economic success, which brings with it college education for their children. There are other incompatibilities. The parents are doers; the youth is an observer who wants to emphasize (at least to *their* face) his reflective nature. He demonstrates a desire to be detached, questioning, and tentative—to be a somewhat contemplative person, who values thought as much as action, who unashamedly slows down, looks around, even at times gazes, turns ideas over and over and around and around, and *wonders*.

With his friends the same youth can be different, in fact openly and naturally like his father. Because he wants to be his father's son, but also his own man, the youth must confront his father in various ways, politely sometimes and rather insistently at other times. The use of marijuana could easily fit into such a youth's life, to accommodate his struggles and purposes. Many young men and women have found marijuana a helpful means of bringing out what is, anyway, very much part of them at this stage of their lives: a certain sense of detachment; a certain pleasure in mulling over various matters, wondering what will become of the world and, not incidentally, oneself; and a certain willingness to slow down, stop and look, question, think and take ample time for those thoughts. The intent here is neither to dwell only on these differences or points of friction between parents and their children, nor to "explain" the use of marijuana as a result of those frictions. The intent is, rather, to point out that many youths, who experience longings and fears, develop attitudes and sensibilities that can, given the chance, find in marijuana an additional source of expression and even support.

This fulfillment through marijuana, described somewhat abstractly above, is put into forceful, concrete words by a young college student, who tells what "a little grass" does for her:

I smoke with my friends, and my boy friend, and his friends. It's not really to be sociable. It's because we want to be more natural and honest, and it's hard to be that way—the way you are when you're alone and doing some thinking—when you're with other people. I honestly wish my parents would take grass with me. Then we'd settle some of these things, I believe we would. They would stop for a minute and *think*; and I wouldn't feel we were in two different worlds, them and me. I try to talk with them, but they want to talk about facts—about grades, and money, and what a boy's father *does*. I try to get them to sit back, and relax, and smile—I mean smile at themselves, and me, and this whole sad, funny world. But my mother begins to get nervous, and she wants to know why I'm so *philosophical*. When they heard I was using marijuana—I told them—they blamed everything on that. How silly can you get? They said I was in a "daze" a lot of the time, and I was becoming a "radical" in politics, and I wasn't taking good care of myself: I wasn't as neat as I used to be, especially my hair—it's stringy—and I wear sandals all the time, and blue jeans, and a dress practically never. I told them that everything they were saying—*everything* —had nothing to do with smoking grass. I reminded them that they'd been criticizing me all the time about all of those things, and more, and that I'd only tried grass a few months ago; and that, if anything, I was less up-tight than before, and so I could talk easier with them.

No, I don't believe that marijuana solves your problems. How could it? All I claim is that sometimes a few of us get together; we turn on and we enjoy it—we really do. We don't want to take heroin, or cocaine, or LSD, either. Why does everyone say we're going to do that—everyone who's never tried smoking grass? I can't believe what I read about marijuana—what people say, what my own parents say. How can anyone believe the most obvious lies and crazy exaggerations? Wouldn't you be insulted if someone came and told you that because you have a drink or two every *week*—not every day—that you'd soon be a drug addict, and uncurable, the way addicts are? That's what my dad said; he said I'd soon be taking worse drugs, and I'd lose all my "values and goals." I jumped him on that. I told him that's what I wanted; I wanted to talk with him about my values and his, my goals and his. But he dropped it like a hot potato; he just kept on telling me how *dangerous* marijuana is. I think it's more dangerous that he and I can't talk honestly, and that he believes only what he wants to believe, what he reads—stuff written by people who cater to his prejudices, rather than give him sensible information and try to challenge him to go find out things for himself, and be his own judge of what's true and what's false.

In a ghetto many youths—far poorer than the young lady above and far less interested in long, elaborately worded discussions—are faced with not altogether different worries and complaints. Poor youths also struggle to be themselves, to find their particular destiny, and to define values they can live with and fall back upon—believable values, not the words, words, words that make up fake and insulting pieties. The following interview is with a young man of seventeen, who is neither an enthusiastic talker nor a self-styled observer of the human condition. Nevertheless at times he bursts forth with wry social comment and angry impatience at the self-righteous dishonesty he sees all around. He also boasts of using marijuana, which he somehow finds helpful, although he does not necessarily recommend it for everyone:

I don't tell my dad to smoke. I don't tell my mother, either. Why should they? It's not their thing. They know I do. They don't care, so long as I don't go into the hard stuff. My father says so long as I work hard, like I'm doing, he knows I'm not into the hard stuff, and he knows I'm alright with pot. They're not me, and most of the time they know it. Sometimes the old man will lose his temper and tell me what it was like for him when he lived in Alabama; but now he's here, and most of the time he's too busy janitoring to worry about me and my brothers. He just keeps his eye on us, he says, but he doesn't worry. He says when he starts to worry, we'll hear about it—fast. My mother works in the hospital, in the laundry department there. She comes home tired, real tired. Man, does she sweat in that place. They don't pay her a whole lot, but it's better than not having any money except what my father brings in. Between the two of them, we can eat and pay the rent.

I work, too. I work in the department store. I'm in the stockroom, and it's a lot of lifting, especially the linoleum. I have to carry the rolls from the stockroom to the floor and back again. I have to cut the linoleum to order, and roll it up, and wrap it up. I have to carry it out to the cars or carry it to the shipping department, if they don't want to drive away with it in their cars. They tell me—they've promised me—I'll be a salesman one day. Then I can take orders and collect a commission on each one, and someone else will do the lifting, and the cutting, and the carrying.

I get home and I'm tired. Man, am I tired. I fall onto my bed and I'm dead—I'm dead, man. Then I wake up and I start eating, and it's hard to stop. My mother says I'm like the big machine they have in the laundry; I just take more and more inside me until she's afraid I'll ruin myself from too much, eating up too much. We'll be looking at the TV, and I'll be eating, you know. It's after that, if I go out and see my girl, and we go to the poolroom—it's then that I'm likely to take a joint, just

120

one. It's all I need; yes it is. I'm better at pool with a little high from the joint. I can't say why. My girl, she says I get cool, really cool, but I don't feel too different, maybe a little smarter, a little. I don't *need* it—the joint. I just take it or leave it. I take it because it relaxes me. If I was home, like my dad, watching the TV or putting the barrels out for the garbage people, I wouldn't want a joint, no. I take it with my girl. I take it, like I said, playing pool. I dig it; I dig pot. I'm not an addict. That's crazy, crazy talk. I know who becomes an addict. I know how that happens. If you know the kids before they start with drugs, you can tell which way they're headed. My dad pointed out some kids five years ago to me and said they'd be drunks and addicts before long, before very long. He was right. You know why? He knows them. He knows what they come from. So do I. That's crazy—telling me I'm going to be using the needles—that's crazy. I like beer. I like pot. I like pool and, most of all, I like to take my girl and be with her. That's the best of all your recreations; yes it is. Margie loves a joint. She says it lifts her spirits up. She gets real warm. She gets hot. I get the same way. What's that got to do with taking the hard stuff?

I'm no teacher, and like that. I never finished high school, I didn't. But I'll let you in on something, man: a friend of mine who hits the veins, he started with beer, that's right. He was sipping beer before he ever got himself a joint. He was getting his kicks with beer, and the more he could get, the more he drank up. Sure, he tried pot, but he was going someplace else—don't you see?—and he got there. I used to go to school with him (way in the beginning, in the first or second grade, I think it was) and he was in bad shape then, real bad shape. His mother beat him bad, and he'd show me what she did—his skin all cut up. She used a buckle. Damn woman! His father never was around. He was no good, no damn good. He was always high; his arms were covered with the needlemarks.

I'd like to get the hell out of here. I'd like to live in a nice town, like you see on TV, like the salesmen in the store do. I hear tell black families are moving in, slowly—I hear the salesmen talk. They're not too happy, the salesmen; I hear them when they don't know I'm listening. They shut up when they see me near them. I think if maybe they took a little pot—the salesmen —we could have some real good talking. We could put all the cards down, yes, and see what happens. We do okay together. I work with them, and they're polite to me. My father says it wouldn't have been like that a few years ago. Maybe. How am I to know? My father says I don't know what it was like back in his time, when he was my age. I guess you never do; you only know your own thing. I like to think about what it'll be like later on, for my kids, when they're as old as I am. It'll be better, I believe that. You *have* to believe that. I'll sometimes get to feeling a little good on pot, and I'll say to Margie that the worst is over—the worst the black man has to go through is over. She's not so sure; but you have to feel confident sometimes, even if it's only for a few minutes! There are some times I can know I can be confident. In church we have a minister who gives you that confidence. He's always giving sermons on "confidence."

Then, there's Margie; she makes me feel there's hope for someone like me. She's a girl who wants to better herself, and that's what I believe we should do, if we can find the way. We'll be smoking, and you get to thinking. You dream up how you'll live later on. When you're young you can dream, my mother says, and she's right. You have to dream, especially when you're working so hard, and you're ready to quit. You have to hold onto yourself and dream about later on, when it'll get better. A lot of people are out to block you. A lot of people are crooks and liars, but all dressed up in fancy clothes, and smooth talking, full of smooth talk, and full of themselves—they're that more than anything else. But you can't let them block you. Smile, you smile; and say to yourself that you know what you want, and you'll get it. I'd like to be selling, instead of lifting. I'd like to have Margie as my wife and we'd have kids, and we'd have a home where you could see a tree—at least one—and some grass around us. Yes, that's my dream. That's your answer: Margie and I, we'll smoke a joint and we'll dream together. That's what it's about, when we take a joint. It's no answer—pot—like our minister says, and I agree. But hell, what's the matter with dreaming up the answer in your mind some of the time, in between doing your job, and saving for the day—the time you'll be all set to go and do something, grab your dream and have it, right there in your hands, where you can touch it and it's real. And you don't lose it, you don't let it go through your fingers; no sir, you don't.

This youth demonstrates an almost uncanny mixture of determinism, skepticism, faith, severe doubt, ambition, and barely concealed apprehension. Black and Mexican-American youths, in their struggles to grow up, meet a world traditionally unfriendly—often cruel, mean, and exploitative in a million ways. Yet they and other ghetto youths, no less than middle-class youths, are all too often lumped together for convenient reference, without regard to the wide range of experiences, preferences, and intentions they have or want to have. This particular youth is not a completely "representative" example of black youth, or ghetto youth, or youth who use marijuana; hopefully, no young man or woman is that. No one—no one person at all—can speak for thousands, or millions, of other human beings.

The words of this particular youth somewhat dispel the familiar view of ghettoes as places where marijuana is a mere stepping-stone to hard narcotics—where every despairing youth is ready and willing to succumb to those needles, which one after another offer a shorter and shorter lease on a kind of euphoria, however sad and costly it may turn out to be. Unquestionably there is much despair in the ghettoes; and many do indeed grab at marijuana desperately, then grab at other drugs, even more desperately. And unquestionably, there is enough unhappiness in our suburbs, too—if less obvious, or simply less vulnerable to documentary inspection. Indeed, many suburban youths inhale grass with a kind of surly or frantic insistence that is itself never appeased, not by grass and not by the harder drugs.

123

Drugs and Youth

Obviously, drugs such as LSD or heroin are far more dangerous than marijuana. The reasons underlying their use by the young are urgent, sad, and desperate—not easily placed in one or two neat psychological or sociological categories. In the ghetto, some youths hunger after drugs at the age of nine, ten, or eleven, and others never will. Yet the closeness of their family structure or the level of poverty in which they live are not totally reliable indicators of which child will take to drugs. "I'm smart," a ghetto "child" of thirteen said. "I'll push the stuff, but never take it. Let others go kill themselves with the stuff." He has no father, and his mother is a tired, weary, and sometimes abusive woman, who is on welfare. Yet the boy abstains from heroin, while others succumb tragically. Among middle-class youths there is an alarming, frightening rise in the use of heroin, also with complex causes.

Perhaps the following explanation does some justice to the problem's complexity. Against a background of ever more available dangerous drugs, a background of social and cultural changes in middle-class American life, reflected by words such as *affluence, permissiveness,* and *boredom,* and a background of the much-advertised magical properties of many different pills and foods—some youths, psychologically vulnerable for this or that reason, take up drugs. They may be lonely, sad, anxious, fearful, or extremely unstable. They may be susceptible to the pressures of other users, who are, like a herd, similarly susceptible and pressured. They may be ignorant, naive, silly, thoughtless, sullen, or angry. They may be intent on hurting themselves or their parents or on achieving happiness— some ineffable contentment, some dreamed-of solace.

In other times such youths might have drunk themselves to extinction or risked death with race cars or motor bikes. Some still use those alternatives to escape, to find oblivion, and to express sorrow, bitterness, confusion, and rage—emo-

124

tions that can take the form of indifference and lethargy, or a kind of senseless, teasing (and self-teasing) bravado. But each youth is an individual, and no easy generalizations can be made. Dozens and dozens of hysterical commentators (some of them doctors, not always the easily blamed newspaper reporters) tell the public in a single-minded way why the young take drugs—rather than how the gamut of youths give many different kinds of expression to their various wishes, fears, and worries.

A sixteen-year-old young man—white and of a well-to-do family—who has repeatedly tried heroin, tells his reasons for doing so:

I'm hung up. Am I! I've always been. I mean, I've been in trouble all the way, starting in the first grade, my father says. I don't know what's the matter with me. I just have something ticking away inside of me—dynamite, it is. I take grass and it cools down. I've tried a lot of things, *anything,* to feel quiet inside. I like to sit and feel stretched out—relaxed as I can.

If I couldn't put my hands on grass, I'd try scotch, but I don't like it. I take my dad's car up to ninety, and I feel good that way. But I don't have a license, and I've been caught twice. No point going to jail.

Some will use the stuff and some won't. I can tell who will and who won't. You know yourself when you see yourself in the next guy; and when you don't, you don't. I'm no addict. Maybe I'll become one some day; I don't know. Sometimes I think I'd rather be an addict than be all jazzed up inside, and itching to go someplace, but not knowing where. It beats me why more people take drugs these days—I mean, I don't know the answer to your question. A teacher told me that a long while ago when they didn't have drugs I'd have been put in the stockade for something else. Maybe he's right.

Perhaps the youth's teacher was indeed right. Maybe at certain moments in history, youths already agitated, troubled, forlorn, or wayward—the descriptive words go on and on—do

125

find particular methods of dealing with, revealing, symboliz-
ing, demonstrating, and communicating their thoughts and
feelings. And maybe in those historical moments, particularly
those characterized by change and uncertainty, the rest of us
fail to understand what that young man was trying to say—
how troubled he has been for a long time, and how inevitable
his habit seemed. In viewing drug use, we need to keep a
steady perspective. We do not owe either the troubled user of
drugs or ourselves an abusive, apocalyptic hysteria in which we
lose our sense of history, our knowledge of human development, and, worst of all, the ordinary common sense that even
a seriously hurt and frightened youth, ready to risk heroin addiction, can reveal in remarks like those quoted above.

In the following discussion of what marijuana can have
to do with hurt, sorrow, and spite, it is important to keep an
open mind—really to listen to the young *individuals* and judge
them, if necessary, on that basis, whether in regard to their
use of marijuana or other habits and beliefs.

What
marijuana
does to
the mind

What indeed is to be said about how marijuana influences the mind? How much or how little is known about the psychological effects or psychiatric complications that some doctors insist are serious and damaging and others insist are mild, barely noticeable, and slight? Of course, the psychological reactions caused by marijuana vary, depending upon which person in which frame of mind takes what amount of the drug under what set of circumstances. This variety of response, seemingly only common sense, is nevertheless ignored by too many so-called authorities or propagandists, who unreservedly declare that marijuana does this or doesn't do that, causes one thing or leads to another. But what kind of marijuana? In what amounts? Taken in what way? Used with whom, and by whom, and for what purpose?

The medical and psychiatric literature in this regard, as is not uncommon, has its contradictions and confusion. After all, there is a wide range of human responses to drugs, which in turn are taken in a wide variety of doses, and for a wide variety of reasons—all of which is, finally, written up by physicians and psychiatrists who themselves have cause to see only a limited number of patients, a more limited number of youths, and an even more limited number of marijuana users. At the risk of seeming to take a bland, uncritical posture, we say that some of the sharpest, most somber, and alarming estimates made by psychiatrists with respect to the harm marijuana can cause are true; and so are the angry retorts of those who say the drug is by and large benign—certainly no worse than other substances taken in and enjoyed by American youth, not to mention their elders. Any psychiatric judgment is only as good as the clinical cases that presumably alone (without, that is, the pressure of various ideological tenets) make those judgments seem reasonable and clarifying. Before enumerating the psychiatric consequences marijuana can and does set in motion, we prefer to quote some patients from our clinical studies. Among these patients are some who have brushed with the law and gone to jail—one consequence of taking marijuana which has very definite psychological or psychiatric implications. We feel that young men and women who have used marijuana should have the opportunity here to describe their "symptoms," although we will also offer our professional impressions.

"I feel nothing," is the terse, ironic declaration of an eighteen-year-old young woman, a sophomore at a women's college, who had been using marijuana for two years. She was not denying that marijuana affects her and causes things to happen in her mind. She was, rather, trying to communicate how "dead" (her word) she felt herself to be "inside" (again, her word). Although she perhaps felt nothing, she certainly was not at a loss for words:

> I've been using grass for a year or two, maybe three. I don't remember. It all seems like so long ago. Maybe that's why I feel like nothing; maybe that's why my mind is blown—blown to nothing. I don't know why else. I don't know what's happened to me. I can't sleep. I can't eat most of the time. I feel like I'm dissolving.
>
> No, I'm not seeing anything or hearing anything. I wish I was. I'm crazy; but I *hope* I'm not. Maybe I am. Do *you* think I am? My parents think I am. They've been telling me for five years now that I'm doing everything wrong. They found out I was using grass about a year ago, and my father threatened to call the police. Can you believe it? That's what he said. My mother told me he'd never do it; that he was mad. "Only mad," she said, and that's why he made the threat. I believe he would have—he really would have—if my mother hadn't talked him out of it. Poor mother, my poor mother! That was one of the few times she's ever stood up to him on anything. She told him she'd leave if he called the police. Imagine that! My little sister heard her say it. She said she heard him agree not to say it again— that he'd turn me in to the cops. Then he swore at me. He called me every name you can imagine, my sister said—"that no-good hippie, full of drugs" and all the rest. He was probably drunk!
>
> Using grass was good. I'd feel good. My friends said I looked better when I turned on. Nothing much really happened at first; the very first time nothing at all happened. I do remember that the second or third time I got dizzy. I kept on thinking of a day I spent up in the mountains with my first boyfriend. It was as if I was carried back to that, to him, and I couldn't help myself. I mean, there I was with my friends, with a boy I liked a lot better than the kid I went out with in high school—but I couldn't seem to get it out of my mind, that day we climbed up the mountain, the two of us. I finally told them, my friends, what was on my mind. And they said with

grass you get like that sometimes; your mind stalls on a thing you've gone through, or you look at something and you see it in a new way, like you never have before.

Actually, most of the time grass doesn't do anything drastic to me. It doesn't bring up memories and it doesn't make me stare at the wall, at a picture, and all that. If I'm feeling good, I feel a little better with grass. If I'm feeling bad, I feel worse—a lot worse. I don't feel anything now. I feel nothing—so maybe that's why the grass I took the other day really knocked me out bad, real bad. I felt so bad just after I took it that I wanted to go kill myself. It was as if there was something in the grass that got into my head and was telling me to go jump out a window, or turn the stove on. I didn't even have the strength to tell my friends what was wrong. I sat there and they said I was really "in myself," and I didn't answer; and then they said it again. And then, when I still didn't answer, they said I was "tripping" real bad and maybe had taken LSD. But I didn't. I was just "psyching"—"psyching" very bad. Now I'm over that. Now my mind is gone. I wonder where it went to. I wish I knew. Do you know what it's like to have no mind? Maybe my father did it after all. Maybe he called those cops, and they came and took my mind away, and maybe it's locked up someplace.

I called home and asked my mother if she knows where my father and his friends, the cops, had put my mind; and poor mother, she got very, very upset. She told me to stop joking like that. I told her, no, I wasn't joking. She said I must be. Then she changed her mind and said it was the drugs, all the drugs I was taking—they were making me think crazy, and talk crazy. Maybe she's right. I said no, though, it wasn't the drugs. It was that my mind just left me, and I'm going to try to find it; and if they can help, I'd be very grateful to them, even to my father. I'll give him some Acapulco Gold and teach him how to use it; and man, he'll go high, way high, and they won't know him in the office. They'll say the old man has learned how to smile. The old man is a young man. The old man has loosened up; he really has. He's not so lousy tight anymore—so tense, all sewed up and buttoned up and slicked down, real neatlike and shiny and polished, and ready to deposit his checks, and invest his cash, and pay off his mortgages and loans, and call himself totally solvent, and then drop from a heart attack (which is the first time a lot of people like him ever know they have a heart, a real, honest-to-goodness heart). But by then it's too late. By then you can't be free anymore. I think it's too late for me, too.

This young woman slipped into a confused, excited, anxious state—into a world of excessive fears and hard-to-justify suspicions. Doctors could call her psychotic, but no medical or psychiatric terminology captures the sense of emptiness and loneliness that a patient like her can so briefly and directly convey with those three words: "I feel nothing." She actually felt a lot, rather obviously, and she could speak what she felt, but she also was thoroughly detached. She spoke about seemingly painful, saddening, and dismaying matters with a kind of distance, an indifference almost, that seemed, even to her, strange and deathlike—what Emily Dickinson in one of her poems has described most pointedly and eerily in the phrase "zero at the bone." There is indeed something chilling—chilling beyond any words—to the kind of "slow madness," as she called it, that young lady was experiencing. She wondered whether marijuana somehow hadn't set it all in motion—perhaps brought something out that may have been *in* her, but now was *all over* her, seizing her every word and thought, wearing her down, turning her into a person without feelings (a person actually very much with feelings, but not pleasant or hopeful feelings, only bitter and somber ones).

In commenting on the relationship between her psychological difficulties and her use of marijuana, few, if any, psychiatrists would say that those difficulties were caused by marijuana—or, for that matter, by any one particular person, event, or thing. In this instance, a young lady with plenty of worries, angers, and disappointments chose to use marijuana for awhile. As the above interview illustrates, however, marijuana and its various psychological effects were by no means her chief "problem," if that is the proper word. Months of interviews with this young woman disclosed the very real and serious tensions, in connection with friends, that she had felt for years. The use of marijuana undoubtedly made her more vulnerable at times. That is, the use of marijuana made her more vividly, more bluntly, and more thoroughly aware of her particular (and overwhelming) feelings, her moods, and her struggles; but it would be difficult to blame the drug for them or, for that matter, for the severe psychological crisis that eventually resulted in hospitalization and prolonged psychotherapy.

In fact, when the various statements about marijuana made by psychiatrists—as well as by many users—are assembled and analyzed, there is less disagreement than would seem. The strongest psychiatric case against the use of marijuana is the same point made by the young lady quoted above: if the user is already depressed and anxious, perhaps verging on a breakdown of sorts, marijuana can give his state of mind a more explicit and overwhelming psychological presence.

The above statement presumes a relatively moderate dose of marijuana—an amount that in different circumstances can bring out quite different feelings, such as a sense of relaxation or a spirit of quiet contemplation. Marijuana "laced" with other drugs or taken in particularly heavy dosages can cause any number of severe medical and psychiatric symptoms. An obvious danger is that no one knows quite what he or she is getting when something called "marijuana" is obtained from a friend, a neighbor, or a pusher. The illegal drug can be contaminated with all sorts of harmless or extremely dangerous substances and thus can be mild or very powerful. Some youths take marijuana for years and suffer no apparent effects, so that one wonders whether they are using anything more than a highly diluted, essentially inert version of the drug. On the other hand, some users describe definite and (to them) unnerving consequences, which may be the result of contaminants in the marijuana, or, alternatively, the result of especially strong marijuana or of an encounter between a psychological vulnerability and the drug. Marijuana apparently brings out "what is already there in the head," as some youths put it, or perhaps "mental status" in medical terminology.

In regard to psychological reactions, marijuana affects the central nervous system rather quickly, though in a variable way and for variable lengths of time—up to three or four hours usually. It both excites and depresses, tones down, or dampens the mind. Thus, marijuana tends to make less influential the part of the mind that broods, worries, and concerns itself with the rights and wrongs of the world, with what ought to be done, and with what might happen if something isn't done. In addition, it slows down ordinary reflexes, just as alcohol does. The subject may not react physically as quickly or as smoothly as usual; that is, he may be less active and less coordinated. On the other hand, the part of the brain that *thinks*—that reflects about the world and responds to people and the emotions they demonstrate—can be stimulated. The user therefore can subjectively feel more alert, more "alive," more sensitive, and more responsive to the world, to other people, and to himself. Again and again, youths have reported that after taking marijuana "time seems different," with a second seeming to last for a minute and a minute for an hour, and that "distance gets changed," with a nearby object seeming quite far off and an object across the room seeming close at hand. Some youths complain: they feel too

133

light-headed; they get dizzy; they feel "flooded" with words that crave expression and "flooded" with ideas and emotions; they have a sensation of floating; they hear ringing noises in their ears; they see things that aren't there; and they notice things in a new way—a detail of a table, a chair, a painting, or "a whole room" seems different in a strongly emotional way as, say, provocatively haunting, ugly, or frightening. Other youths claim that nothing, absolutely nothing, happens to them when they take marijuana; and still others say they have tried the drug once or twice and felt themselves "going under," losing their grip on things, and becoming nervous, confused, panicky, frightened, and overcome by "a rush of things" in their mind.

What sense is one to make of that? Again, marijuana is the object of diverse medical opinion. Some thoroughly respectable, completely sincere, and experienced doctors and psychiatrists say that marijuana is an eminently dangerous drug: they claim its use is an effort to conceal problems, to mask depression and anxiety, and to cover up or forget serious, plaguing worries and fears. In addition, they say marijuana use stems from a desperate, somewhat childlike desire to obtain through the "magic" of drugs what in truth can only be obtained through deeds and achievements—that is, a sense of self-respect, of personal worth, and of purpose. Furthermore, youths who smoke marijuana, they state, are in or are headed for grave trouble, quite possibly for other drugs, for a mental collapse of some kind, or for a delinquent or criminal life. At the very least (and very importantly) they believe that marijuana can weaken a youth's willfulness; his sense of initiative; his involvement in the world; his ambition and capacity to *do* things, to exert his mind, heart, and soul for his own sake and for the sake of others; and his utterly necessary "defenses" (in

134

other words, undo his already tentative and susceptible ways of dealing with threatening inner tensions as well as with baffling or frustrating demands of the outside world).

In reply, other doctors and other psychiatrists—no less sincere, no less competent, and no less familiar with the many vexing sides to that catchall called "the drug problem"— disagree with their colleagues and say instead that by and large marijuana demonstrably cannot be considered an unequivocally dangerous drug, not when it is taken without apparent untoward effect by so many youths in America. They believe rather that marijuana is a relatively mild drug, an intoxicant of sorts, but in its usual doses (inevitably the comparison is made), neither as dangerous as nicotine, which can cause cancer, or alcohol, which can cause cirrhosis of the liver. They admit that the drug does perhaps cause a passing bit of forgetfulness, perhaps even lapses in logic. The new user of marijuana may either experience very little or nothing subjectively, or become somewhat stumbling and slow as measured by various tests (although interestingly enough, the regular users get their "highs," have the subjective experiences, and, of all things, do better on occasion in certain tests than they did before they used marijuana). In general, they think the use of marijuana is not addictive, does not necessarily lead to the use of other drugs, causes nothing as awful as cancer or cirrhosis of the liver, and tends to bring out the contemplative side of the user rather than (as is often the case with alcohol) the outgoing and aggressive side. A few, a *very* few, physicians even argue that marijuana is used to good effect by certain creative people, both patients and non-patients—men and women who respond to the drug affirmatively, that is, with an increased capacity to see the world imaginatively, sensitively, or subtly.

How are those contradictory lines of observations and

135

thought, no doubt based on different clinical experiences, to be resolved? Once again, we intend here no sly, evasive "consensus," purchased at the price of candor and staked out as a position in order to win approval and avoid criticism. This book is not a tract, a piece of medical, psychiatric, and legal propaganda, to be used by groups or individuals whose concerns are in one way or another polemical. We have no interest in comparing alcohol and nicotine to marijuana, as is so often done. What possible help is it to say that marijuana does not cause cancer of the lung and has not yet done the devastating damage to so many millions of human beings that alcohol has caused—when marijuana instead offers its own danger and causes its own problems? By the same token, what help is it to charge marijuana with almost anything and everything—with causing crime and insanity, with ruining minds, and with undermining our society? Marijuana has been taken, whether only once, occasionally, repeatedly, or frequently, by estimated millions of American citizens, many of whom do not go crazy, do not suffer psychiatric collapses, do not take to stealing and killing, and do in fact live reasonably "normal" and effective lives.

Again, we hope to avoid such categorical descriptions of marijuana users as "sick," creative, immature, criminal, or gifted. The psychological (not to mention moral) character of many people all over this country and the globe is under inspection when a discussion such as this unfolds. It is of course true that some extremely troubled, hurt, and ailing people, some mean and vicious people, some utterly sane, sensible, and competent people, and some genuinely unusual or talented people *all* use marijuana. To further complicate (but also simplify) matters, some of these people do so to bad effect, some to very little if any effect, and some to rather pleasant and innocuous effect —at least from the point of view of the users themselves and that of objective observers.

And again, our purpose in writing this book is not to help bring about the legalization of marijuana or its advancement as yet another cure-all; nor is it to offer the various public officials who oppose marijuana the sanction and support of a few more all too certain and assertive professional men. America today is quite full enough of promises, of panaceas, and of experts who are granted too much blind faith, heard all too uncritically, and called upon with an eagerness that can only measure the real complexity of the problems to be faced. It seems fair to call not only upon ourselves, our medical and legal knowledge, our patients, or, for that matter, drug-fanciers and enthusiasts, but once again upon youths who have had some experience with marijuana. These young people willingly tell what *they* think the drug does to their minds; what *they* have come to know, feel, believe, and find significant about "the drug experience"; and what *they* rate both pro and con about that "experience."

"You asked about what grass does to me," a twenty-two-year-old law student began, with a certain characteristic interest in carefully formulating his thoughts before speaking. He went on:

I'll take grass like I did last night and nothing happens, not a single damned thing. I was tired, washed out after an exam. I went with my girl to a party and we all turned on. I almost fell asleep, my girl said. She kept on nudging me. A week ago, though, I got a great high. She and I took grass alone and we've never been closer. It was a wonderful time for us. We really talked. We really saw things. We felt we were reaching each other. I can't put it in words.

137

He is asked to try to do so and whether, after all, he and his girlfriend needed marijuana to get close, to feel the kind of intimacy he described. He hesitated, wondering whether the question made by implication some skeptical or moral assertion, then continued:

I'd be a fool if I told you that the *only* way my girl and I can make it—can understand each other and feel open to each other—is through grass. Of course, we don't need grass that way, that totally. We like to play music when we're together; that helps with a mood, helps us relax and feel warm and emotional. I suppose we could do without music, too—and the soft couch, and the food we nibble on. You can go on and on, and pretty soon there's you and your woman standing stiff-stark alone without any "supports," or whatever you people call them.

We reply that we do not want to be charged with thinking that way, with reference to "supports." He retorts:

I don't mean *you* in particular; but there's a lot of crazy talk (if you'll forgive the expression) that comes out of "shrinks" —and the lawyers who use "shrinks" in court. My girl and I take pot and say we have a great time; we felt close, real close. And then the "shrink" says we're relying on "supports," on "artificial" things or "magical" things, which means we're not really grown-up, which means we're in danger because we'll escalate— take more and more grass, harder drugs, the works! I've read the articles. Maybe they're right when they describe some mixed-up people or real young kids. But they're unfair to a guy like me. I've used grass on and off now ever since I was a junior in college, and I'm doing pretty good—I believe I am—as is my girl. She's here in the law school. She loves to use grass, occasionally. She feels that it helps her relax and think—that's right, *think*. She's not a child. She's not in need of a "shrink-job." Neither am I. Why do so many people believe that if you use grass you've got emotional hang-ups or you're soon going to be

138

a crook, or crazy, or an addict? It's amazing (when you stop and think how many millions of people have used the drug, right here in America), it's amazing that people don't stop and ask themselves why they jump to those conclusions. Thousands of people get killed because they're driving while drunk, but let one kid get killed because of something even remotely connected to drugs—*any* drug—and people get hysterical. Sure, kids who are mixed-up take drugs and get more mixed-up. They would probably have gotten mixed-up without drugs, without alcohol, without anything, because time goes by and they have more experiences and more pain, and eventually they break—they crack. Isn't that what usually happens? Why take the kids who are going downhill for reasons you know better than me, and then say it's grass, it's grass that did it? If they're going down, they're going down, and they need your help—not grass, but help. But it's ridiculous to say that grass did it—caused the trouble—or even that without grass those kids, those poor kids, would be much better off.

I'm no doctor, and I'm no statistician either. I haven't taken any polls. But I'm a student, and I know a lot of other students. Almost all, almost *all* of my friends have tried grass a few times, and most of them "turn on" about once a month, maybe more, maybe less. We're not crazy. We're not dropouts. We're not without ambition. We're not living in a dream world. We're not turning to crime. We're not getting ready to take heroin, or LSD, or amphetamines, or all the rest. Sure I'm angry. I'm angry at some of the talk I hear from people who've never tried grass; who aren't of my generation; who damn well don't know how we live, what we're doing; and who aren't in the least inclined to leave their offices, leave their patients, and go out and look and listen, and meanwhile stop preaching.

From a medical student came rather similar comments, with a few additional points:

I've used pot for about five years—not too much, just on a weekend, when I want to unwind. It's not the greatest thing, pot, but I like it as much as alcohol—sometimes more, sometimes less; it depends on my mood. I get a pleasant high, then lose it and feel fine—no hangover.

I wish to hell more doctors would try pot before they sound off. I can imagine someone apparently stable getting frightened by the stuff, but that kind of person will get an "anxiety reaction" in church, or on a plane, or in a crowd. They have to stay away from more things than pot. There are always people who can't take something, who are allergic, or unstable, or all the rest. You can poison yourself with aspirin. You can get dizzy, too, and ruin your stomach. Some people aren't grown-up, like the psychiatrists say, so they start in with aspirin, take too much of it, go on to other pain-killers, become addicts, rob to pay for the heroin. But what's the problem there: the aspirin or the individual, the mixed-up individual? Hell, if we want to protect them against all the things they'll succumb to, we'll have to abolish cars, and planes, and tunnels, and crowds, and tall buildings, and all the rest. I've read the literature on marijuana. What you don't see is reports of how people like me use it, year after year. You read about experiments or people who started out with marijuana and ended up in a state hospital or something, but no one goes and talks with hundreds of thousands of students, with my generation. You read about some laboratory tests—when everyone knows that your reaction to the drug depends on where you are, and who you are with, and your mood. You read about the bad things that happen, which are reported by doctors and psychiatrists who naturally see the bad things all day long. *I* don't go to see a psychiatrist. My friends in medical school don't. And we take pot from time to time, we do, and we like it sometimes and get nothing out of it other times; that's how I'd put it. I think an anthropologist and a doctor with no axe to grind (if there are any) ought to go *out,* go out in the "field" and observe—observe a lot more American young people than anyone has so far, to my knowledge. There ought to be that kind of research, so older people could get the information they need—from us, the ones who have the experiences to talk about.

Yet a graduate student, a history major, had this to say:

I've tried marijuana; I've smoked a few joints. It's a big disappointment. Nothing, absolutely nothing, happened to me. I waited and waited. I finally smoked more, then more and more, and at last something *did* happen. My heart started pounding, and I got a bad case of blurring—I couldn't seem to see straight and clear. I was frightened out of my mind. I began to be afraid of the people near me—my own friends! I wanted to go home, real bad. I wanted to be in my room, all by myself, and in bed. It took me a couple of hours to calm down. My boyfriend took me home, and I asked him to leave, but he wouldn't. Soon I was okay. I'll never go through that again. They can have it—marijuana! It's a dangerous drug. I have friends who agree with me. They've become scared; that's what happens when you take it.

No, I've never been to a psychiatrist. I honestly don't believe there's anything wrong with me. Some of the people I know who use marijuana, they're really wild. They've lost all purpose. They're lazy. They're dropouts from society. I'm not afraid to say it. They sit, and sit, and sit. They talk, and talk, and talk. Do they ever do anything? Two of them started graduate school with me and have dropped out. They say they're radicals, but they don't really *do* anything radical. Oh, maybe once or twice a year they march, but they're reacting to what other people have started.

I really believe some of the people I know who use marijuana are—they're like children, spoiled children. They demand, demand, demand. They criticize others all the time, but never look to themselves, their own failures; they're "mean tongues," I'll tell you. They live in their own private world, and they're intolerant of others—and *such* intolerance; it's terrible to see! They're as prejudiced and narrow-minded as all the police, and politicians, and "squares" they dump on all day long. They're as cruel, too —as brutal as the "pigs" they talk about, and less attractive; I'm not afraid to say so. What bothers me is that too many people, at least on this campus, are afraid to criticize them—afraid to come out and say they look dirty, behave unattractively and spitefully, and are a nasty crowd; that's all I can say—nasty! I'm not saying marijuana causes them to be like that, not by itself. But they sure all use it—use a lot of it.

So, there are the claims and counterclaims, experiences of one sort and experiences of another sort, judgments and judgments that take issue with judgments—all a part of an America that increasingly tries to comprehend its growing "drug scene." Hopefully America will examine its drug problem in a way that does credit to its stated desire for two centuries to be a democracy, whose citizens want as much freedom as is consistent with the rights of others. An inherent right of each citizen is protection from various dangers—some obvious and some not so obvious—whether they be harmful drugs, maliciously peddled, or punitive narrowness, a commodity of sorts that also can be maliciously peddled.

Flying high
or low

Blacks and Puerto Ricans have always furnished the large majority of traditional addicts, and they still do. Today nearly three out of every four addicts are black, and over half of all the nation's addicts live in New York City. As explained previously, it is impossible to know the exact number of addicts in the United States, but estimates range from fifty thousand to over half a million, in any event far less than our six million alcoholics. The black addicts are poor, often recent arrivals from the South; they are dazed inhabitants of the ghetto who often begin with pep pills or pot at age ten or twelve. Middle-class parents shudder at this, perhaps more from abstract or moral outrage than from concrete realization of what in fact makes a child in elementary school welcome a reefer. Ironically, the drug use that formerly marked ghetto youths now exists among college students and suburban youths. It is as if the exiled poor (and some militant bohemians, who always experimented with pills and drugs) have now found, at least in one respect, common cause with "solid America."

We recently observed a poor ghetto family as they watched a television documentary on drugs. One of the children, an eight-year-old boy, had participated in the television program, which also explored the psychological and educational effects on black children of being bussed across the city to white schools. (The children call the rides "cross-town trips.") The family has six children, all but one of whom sleep in the same room. The mother is on relief, and the father is rarely seen. The father was once a drug addict, and his wife's opinion of "trips," not surprisingly, strongly contrasts with that of middle-class youths. Her commentary after the television program was recorded:

That's the big laugh, them college kids playing around with them reefers and trying to get their thrills. It's like in civil rights, though. You need the rich white man to get himself hurt before anyone pays attention. I wish they'd come out here, those boys, and have a few for us, and let us go live the way they do. Because I'll tell you, no one around here would be looking for kicks if they had something better, and now they try to tell you that if you do get something better, then your kids turn right around and they look for the same kicks we do. But I don't believe it, because they must be just a few. Me, if I had the money I'd go get their father and he'd have the doctor he's supposed to have. They'd fix up his stomach so it don't bleed anymore, and then he wouldn't come telling me he has to keep the habit, or he'll die of pain, and besides, there's nothing else to do, so that's it. I tell him, better to stay and help me around, but he says he couldn't face being another kid, so he goes off and he gets high and he feels like a big shot. If we had the money, he'd *be* one, a real-life big shot, and no fooling and kidding himself and bragging to the boys that he can fly higher than the capsules and he's been to the moon first, before anyone else, and then crying and saying no, he only flies low. To me, the money would solve a lot—I mean not just the place we live and that, and the food, but I mean it would bring Frank home, and he'd kick the habit for good, and no college kid would tell him he's crazy for being square, and not free and easy. Because Frank, he'd say to them: "Look boys and girls, don't come telling me about it. I been there way before you, and longer, and you can have it, every lousy stinking cloud, and the moon, and everything, because I want a place to land, like you've got, and when I get it, that's the end of flying for me, and you can have it, and stay up there all you want."

This woman's message, condensed from a much longer conversation, is clear and is the same as that of her husband. Years before marijuana or LSD became the subjects of middle-class debate, he was smoking reefers. He had eventually gone the mainline route of heroin and cocaine, in addition to a heavy intake of beer and wine ("water" he called them). Twice he had been hospitalized, and twice he returned to drugs. He is presently off them and hopes the third "clean time" will be the last:

It better be, or I'll be gone. I almost was when they found me, but God made the hospital get me before the police could. With the police, you lose blood. They beat you so hard you get to take a trip just taking their fists. But in the hospital they cleaned me out good, and I'm trying to stay like that. They got me to a place where they're teaching me work, and I figure if I ever get a job, I'll be ready to go home, and we can tell welfare to go spy someplace else. But to be honest I can't trust myself, and I don't think I'll be able to stay clean. There's a lot like me, and we don't like it, but you know how it goes, you find a door and you take it, and so every time you're just sitting around and getting nowhere, someone starts pushing you, and there's the door, and you know you can leave and get away, so you do before you know it. You don't think, it just happens, like the light's out, and then it's on, and then you have to keep the juice going, or it'll go out, and, that's where you meet the cops, stealing. But, I'll tell you, I never want to be there; if you asked me, I'd say, "come on in and bring me back, if you can find the way." But by yourself, it's hard. So I hope my boy takes that school serious; sometimes I even hope he gets lost, and some big-rich family over there, the white folks you know, get ahold of him and try the integration thing, maybe, with him in their house. Then I'd know one of us at least took to a better way out than I did, and that's the truth.

It is difficult to reconcile the "escape" that drugs offer this man with the "release of freedom" students claim to have from grass or acid. Many ghetto youths find marijuana not an exciting path to "self-discovery," but an inevitable aspect of a fierce and brutish life that is not conceptualized but lived—"every goddam minute," as the mother just quoted expressed it when relating the regularity of her various worries. When ghetto youths, who at fourteen or fifteen are aging fast, are asked what drugs do for them, they are puzzled by and impatient with the outside interest: "What you mean? Why do you take the car fast or spin your records? If you go get yourself some real kick, is that bad?" "If you don't, you lose out and there's nothing, that's my opinion." "You itching to take a smoke, but scared?"

On the other side of the ghetto wall, tight, self-conscious, well-to-do students, whose circumstances ghetto and poor youths eye with envy, tell psychiatrists that the world is bad, rotten, evil, hypocritical and must at all costs be fled. The theme on campus, as in the ghetto, is escape, but the trips are different. The college youths give wordy and self-congratulatory descriptions of their departure through drugs, in contrast to the silence, sullenness, or half-hearted anger evident in the ghetto youths who are "gone" from the nowhere of cold, dreary, rat-infested tenements. Put differently, race, class, money, and power haunt the drug scene too.

146

Fake morality, which appalls students high on pot or acid, does not belong exclusively to the bourgeois world. The following claims are often heard in the bourgeois drug world: marijuana helps one to expose hypocrisy and dishonesty; and LSD provides "an impetus toward self-actualization," or "increased self-awareness, self-acceptance, religious feeling and reorientation of values," as Masters and Houston described it in *The Varieties of Psychedelic Experience*. (The same old Lady Jargon, plying her seductive banalities in new territory.) In any event, it is doubtful that black, poor youths find "self-actualization" (whatever the term is meant to convey) through drugs, even though many of them have tried all kinds of trips by themselves and in "groups" (admittedly without psychological scrutiny and scientific or religious leadership). Drugs have yet to provide an empirical, or existential, consensus that transcends the concrete facts of everyday life—a failure that should trouble only naive transcendentalists, some of whom "tune in, turn on, and drop out" with a passionate and confident sense of direction that no doubt could force a scornful laugh from a statue of Buddha.

The American social and economic system, which makes the ghetto possible, apparently finds vindictive legislation against addicts easier to accomplish than any real effort to change tenement life in the ghetto. Ghetto youths, high on pot, yearn for the very things that college acidheads decry. Negro children draw pictures of big, flashy Cadillacs filled with bottles of cola, cookies, and oversized heaters. They persist in mixing their metaphors, confusing their goals, and resorting to materialistic symbols (which many affluent liberals detest and see as evidence of exploitation of the poor, who are described as identifying with the "aggressor"). But the people of the ghetto are not only brainwashed victims of advertising

147

agencies and the news media. They have to eat and pay rent, and to do so they have to make money or, failing that, check in regularly with the welfare department.

The middle-class citizen, the "aggressor" who easily keeps the poor in their place, has his troubles on occasion in controlling his own brood. Middle-class youths reject all that they have in order to "turn on," spurning not only their parents but the entire American "character" or "system." Well-to-do students devastate with criticism the work-bound automatons, guilt-bound analysands, and church-bound immoralists who would destroy another race, another country, and even the whole planet to keep America as it is today—first and foremost, a sanctuary for the like-minded. One of these students put it on the line to his psychiatrist:

Psychiatrists are more—or you could say less—than doctors treating people who are "sick," and if they don't know it, they're idiots. In this country they're priests to the middle-class atheists who are so confused and frightened they don't dare call themselves atheists. They keep on telling themselves and everyone else to "adjust," to find out what "reality" is and then "cope" with it. How's that for a conservative's dream—the doctors say you should do business with us, so you'd better, or you'll be unhealthy, and we'll have to give you vitamins, in a state hospital. Why don't psychiatrists say that the healthy man is the one who wants to change things, so the world is different, and we think differently, and get along differently.

Is this young man, after all, a disillusioned activist taking time out to drop out, yet ready to storm any barricade that seems even remotely available and approachable? Are drugs his "realistic" alternative, taken at a time of retrenchment, when the skirmishes in the South and the slums have given way to a real, honest-to-goodness war? The young man laughs a little too much at this idea, almost relieved to hear exactly

148

what he expected. "No. I don't mean change the way you do," he said sharply:

No. I don't mean "behavioral change," or even "societal change." I mean a change of eyes and heart. You people, you'll give someone glasses, or you stick an electrode in his heart and make the same muscle go on and on. Or you tell a guy he needs therapy, so he comes into the office, and what does he see: a few sail boats, or a picture by a famous artist, the real thing if you've been in practice for a long time, or only a reproduction if you're just starting out. Then we start talking, and every time we tell you something, you call attention to it, and call it a name, and compare it to what other people do. And which other people? People like you, the next-door neighbors. There are passive-aggressive relationships, and sado-masochistic ones, and immature or infantile ones, and symbiotic ones, and irrational ones, and abnormal ones—so that you get the feeling a few "mature" ones exist, in some psychiatric hothouse, where a "seal of approval" is given, after ten years of evaluation and analysis, round the clock.

Then a guy takes pot, and tries to look inside himself, and see what's going on, what he feels, and what it all means, the country we've got, and how we live—and you guys are right there, waiting. You tell us it's dangerous, we'll get hooked on worse things, and spend the rest of our lives tied down—to drugs, not to making money and paying mortgages and getting ahead in the psychiatric profession. Or you say we're "disturbed," or "neurotic" or "latent psychotics," because we're being "passive" and "withdrawn," and we don't cut our hair the way you do, and we think neckties don't mean anything, and we have "anti-social tendencies" because we become violent over lynchings and war, and you believe in non-violent accommodation to slums, napalm and all the rest. We're supposed to get with it, get "mental health," become "well-adjusted"—to what? And if we try to talk to one of you guys about some of this, we get that benevolent look, or a kind of smug and damn unfriendly stare, as if to say "That's o.k., kid, I understand, you're just getting your kicks, as we all do when we're *growing up*." Those are the words that

149

tell the most, as if some tired old guy sitting on his rear end in an office, selling time and raking in a large bag of money every day doing it, has *got* to have the truth about *growing up,* when all he does is sit down, but no sit-ins, because that's "acting out." It's a fool-proof system you've got: disagree with me and you need help.

This young man exhibits the very theoretical or conceptual tendency (no matter for what purpose) that he and other college students often abhor in themselves and others. A ghetto youth high on pot is likely to express—if indeed he talks at all—worries, fears, and anger. He may experience sex, not because it is released in some sudden flood, but because it is there, waiting and available. Altogether he is likely to withdraw rather than, as suburban and college youths describe it, to "fuse" with an idea, a concept, or a person.

One ghetto man related a sense of "flying high" while on drugs:

Well, it's not really a plane, but a car, man. I put wings on my car and go up, and ride along the street here, but the hell with the traffic and the lights. And I get someplace, because I'm moving along. I feel like I could lean out and take a TV wire in my hand and pull the set right out of the building.

Perhaps this man would like to disembowel those rotting, collapsing buildings; perhaps he is "upset" or "militant." In any event, he is "flying low," close to his life and the feelings that life generates.

Across town old doctrines are denounced and new ones embraced—talk, always talk, from people who say grass will free them from, ironically, the need to talk, to be "uptight," wordy, theoretical, and scholarly. Psychiatrists are condemned as yet another gang of constricted Puritans by people who

150

defiantly proclaim "experiences" that are meant to accuse (whom really?) as much as simply happen.

Acid and pot are sought in the hope that they will burn away at all the middle-class concepts and sophisticated perceptions—all the learned dos and don'ts that pay off year by year in smiles, promotions, and cash. Acid and pot are supposed to burn away at what Freud saw joined: civilization and its discontents. The loudest advocates of grass—its propagandists rather than casual clients—want it to enter the lungs and then the blood, to go to the "highest" layers of the cortex and weaken what is called at clinical conferences "the mind's structure"—what is shared by vulgar psychiatrists and brazen generals, student activists and acidheads, some of whom also can be vulgar or brazen. They want the vindictive, rule-bound self to lose its nerve. The earnest, compliant self that works hard and is loyal to stop signs and speed limits might become a victim of the very images, fantasies, and dreams it usually controls—more or less, depending on the person, the time of the day, and the circumstance. Joy and visions might emerge, and excited horror. Yet, in truth, through all the drug experience the mind's accumulated property, capital, experience, "structure," sophistication—whatever—are given up, a process of surrender that is an inevitable part of the drug scene for those who have something but want to give that something up. In our society strippers are well paid, and certainly they are not beggars.

It is claimed that a reefer is cheaper than an analytic hour—that grass or acid probes farther and works faster. But certainly a user can take grass or acid and face no one and nothing, except his aloneness. Nietzsche insisted that it "takes two to make a truth." If a person uses drugs to find truth,

to be free, and in so doing becomes quite literally more isolated, more taken up with his own vision and voice—then
how much truth has he found; how free is he?

In any event, there are two distinct drug scenes—that
of the poor and desperate, and that of the comfortable and
dissatisfied—and the distance that separates them is as great
as the one that separates them both from their "square"
counterparts. The youths in the ghetto and in the middle-
class schools, colleges, and suburban homes only *seem* a little
closer by virtue of the "drug habit." In fact, they are the
same strangers (and antagonists) the rest of us are. Grass and
acid free them of neither the fears nor the desires that char-
acterize them—as the human beings they inescapably are by
virtue of their past, their lives, and their "condition." No
mind, however jazzed up and "expanded," can lose its own
history—its character as part of a particular body alive in a
particular place and time. The use of drugs does not contra-
dict this obvious and "old-fashioned" truth, but in a curious
way once more demonstrates it.

The law is commonly thought of and commonly thinks of itself
as the means of maintaining stability in a society. The law's
alleged purpose is to prevent people from infringing on the
rights of others—rights the law has decided other people have.
Yet, ironically, all criminal laws are themselves infringements
upon individual freedom. Obviously, limitations on freedom
are necessary if we are to exist as a society. In this country
the history of criminal law in general and of particular criminal laws has been marked by a constant struggle between
the individual's right to a certain degree of freedom and society's right to stability and order. The history of our criminal
justice system illustrates the tension between those two important rights. On one side stands "the state," sometimes
called "the people," personified by the police and the prosecution; and on the other stands the accused, the individual.
In the middle, hopefully, sit the judge and the jury—and

153

before them all come our lawmakers, who presumably balance the interests of every one.

There are certain offenses, such as murder, robbery, and rape, that clearly involve damage or injury to other individuals, but it is more difficult to determine how other so-called offenses are harmful to society. It is more debatable whether fornication, adultery, and homosexual acts consented to by grown people harm society; yet they are prohibited acts, punishable in most states as criminal offenses.

Lawyers, judges, teachers, and legislators often say that the law is not something called "morality," nor should it be. Yet when the law terms fornication and adultery "offenses," it is reflecting moral codes if not prescribing them. The failure in most areas of this country either to enforce such laws or to repeal them illustrates the confused state of our thinking. We are not quite ready to repeal these laws, which are a legacy of our past; yet we ignore them often enough to make farces of them. As a result, millions of "private crimes" are tolerated. Many men untrained in law do not even know they are committing crimes when they cheat on their wives, for example.

Today, use of drugs, whether harmful or not, is also a crime. Those who use harmful drugs argue that if someone wants to kill himself with certain drugs (or "dope," as it used to be called), then so what? Isn't the ultimate in personal freedom the freedom to destroy oneself? Of what interest should it be to the state? Still, suicide continues to be a crime in many states. In medieval England (whence our laws came) the law proudly claimed to be a bulwark to morality; it punished suicide by putting a stake through the dead man's heart and confiscating his land. Although the law has since advanced a little, it is still held that suicide is an evil, but for social rather than moral reasons. The reasoning behind this perhaps reflects upon our

154

morality better than the stake in the heart reflected upon that of medieval England. We say that the man who commits suicide leaves his dependents economic burdens to society or, if he has no dependents, his cadaver to be dispensed with by others, who may not be capable of paying for it. In other words, we say that the death of one man affects each man in a more or less direct economic way. And so it is with self-inflicted deaths whether they are sudden or slow, as in the use of certain drugs. The state thus has shown an interest in preventing suicide and has convinced us that it has a right to intervene. What is more real in America today than the pocketbook?

But why, some ask, should the state be interested in the drugs that don't kill or those that we do not believe harm individuals, if used moderately? If the state has acceptable reasons to keep us from killing ourselves (a point for only philosophers to debate), what is the state to do about laws that keep us from enjoying ourselves—bar us from the "inalienable right" of "the pursuit of happiness," to borrow a seemingly hedonistic phrase from, of all places, the Declaration of Independence?

The federal government, the District of Columbia, and each of the fifty states has its own drug laws. We have many different punishments for violations of these laws. Yet, more Americans are taking more drugs in more ways than ever before because drugs are supposed to offer happiness and freedom, both of which are becoming more evasive and have yet to be defined.

In any event, our federal and state laws dealing with various drugs, particularly marijuana, are in terrible shape, as everyone concerned—governors, attorney generals, legislators, judges, prosecutors, defense attorneys, policemen, and, most of all, defendants—would agree. But such broad state-

155

ments can no longer be made in this section, which will attempt first to set out the many problems the drug laws present to all of us, and second to shed some light on what course to take when one is confronted by these laws.

We live under a federal system made up of fifty separate states, each one of which has separate laws and separate penalties for violations of those laws. In addition to the fifty state systems is a federal system of law, and the District of Columbia also has its own laws. In other words, on any given subject the law can be and often is different in each state, and it also may be different from the federal law. A glance at the next chapter will show how extraordinarily the laws differ from state to state. Unfortunately, little can be done about this diverse legal situation.

The basic legal fact under our federal system is the separation of the fifty states, so that each state can pass its own laws more or less in its own way and establish its own penalties. There is one stipulation, however, that becomes particularly important with regard to the laws and legal procedures relating to drugs. *No state law or legal procedure can be in violation of the United States Constitution.* If a pyramid were to be drawn illustrating the levels of legal power, at the top would be the United States Constitution. All other laws—federal, state, city, or town—must be in accordance with the Constitution. Next in authority come the various state constitutions (in many, but not all, instances virtual restatements of the Constitution) which cannot violate the United States Constitution. State statutes must be in accord with the state constitution as well as the United States Constitution. Below these are local ordinances, or bylaws: "do not park on the left side of the street," for example. Local ordinances also must conform to the federal Constitution and the state constitution in addition to the state laws.

156

Our major concern here will be with state and federal statutes, or laws, and with the United States Constitution.

Although for many years there have been state and federal laws against the use of drugs, prohibition of drugs began with the passage of the Uniform Narcotic Drug Act in 1932, interestingly enough about the time prohibition of alcohol ceased. Basically the law dealt with the sale, use, manufacture, possession, and transfer of "narcotic" drugs. Many states either adopted the act wholesale or varied it to suit themselves.

The Uniform Narcotic Drug Act, which was proposed by the Federal Bureau of Narcotics, assumed without much scientific research or inquiry that marijuana was a narcotic. Until the 1950s few middle-class Americans had any reason to know about narcotic drugs—to know, for instance, that the law hindered research into what marijuana actually is and does. No one could legally possess the drug, and studies of it were not encouraged. Mayor Fiorello La Guardia of New York City in 1938 did commission a study of marijuana that today is generally thought to be inadequate for a number of reasons. Two major defects were that only seventy-seven people were tested and that the researchers examined the effect of only eating marijuana, not smoking it. The La Guardia report was gospel—probably because the laws against its possession prevented marijuana even from being used for research—until fairly recently. Any changes in the law during this period resulted from local, isolated conditions—for example, the death of a youth from an overdose—and were almost invariably in the direction of stiffer penalties, on the assumption that there really was not much difference between marijuana and morphine or heroin. Whether or not it actually is, marijuana is considered to be a narcotic and a harmful drug by the state and federal laws of this country—a discrepancy

157

that accounts for, in essence, the problem of the law and marijuana.

If nothing else, Prohibition taught us that when respect for a law is gone, then the power of that law is also gone. Simon and Garfunkel sing in "Save the Life of My Child": "Kids ain't got no respect for the law these days," and then they add, "blah, blah, blah," indicating their, and no doubt most of their listeners', disdain for such comment. But the facts are that the policeman who says these words has a lot to back him up and the "kids" feel, like Simon and Garfunkel, full of "blah" at outworn pieties. Both the police and those "kids" know that a substantial majority of people ignore and violate a number of certain laws that they have ceased to respect.

Many lawmakers, lawyers, and judges have observed that the harshness of the drug laws, particularly the marijuana laws, has created a lack of respect for the law in general and, in turn, a threat to our whole legal system. According to *Newsweek* and *Time*, the Vice-President's daughter was caught with marijuana at the National Cathedral School for girls. And on 3 December 1969 at the White House Conference of Governors on Drug Abuse, according to the *New York Times,* the daughter of the governor of New Hampshire said, "I don't think there is anything wrong with smoking pot myself." At the same conference, the daughter of the governor of Missouri said, "It's your own thing. I don't understand why someone should be put in jail for smoking marijuana." Lawmakers every day read such comments and on their own observe that young people—middle-class young people—are increasingly taking drugs. Lawmakers know that pot is being sold in colleges, high schools, prep schools, junior high schools, and sometimes grade schools and that even their own children have tried one or another drug. And, for the most part, lawmakers are confused.

The battle over legalization has produced polemics from all directions. Some say that if marijuana is legalized, we'll soon have to legalize heroin, cocaine, LSD, DMT, and STP. Some believe that once it is legalized, the thrill of smoking marijuana will be gone, and our youth, not satisfied with what is legal, will move up the drug ladder. On the other side, the arguments are: prohibiting the marijuana route to the "pursuit of happiness" denies an "inalienable right"; prohibiting a substance that in itself is apparently no more harmful than those already present—alcohol and nicotine—is illogical; it is the liquor and tobacco industries that, from fear they will lose business, are fighting any relaxation of the marijuana laws; and finally, there are legal constitutional arguments against the present laws. For example, some say that to call marijuana a narcotic or harmful drug, as most of our laws do, constitutes an illegal classification: that is, although it is as harmful as marijuana, alcohol is not prohibited, and such a disparity as the law's "failure to prohibit" alcohol violates the Fourteenth Amendment's guarantee of equal protection of the laws. Prohibitions against marijuana are also believed to violate the right of privacy, which the Constitution indirectly guarantees. Even though there is no part of the Constitution which specifically declares "a right to privacy," there *are* parts which recognize that certain activities of the citizens are their own business. This argument, which has been used successfully in cases attacking prohibitions against birth control and the possession of pornography, may one day come to affect our drug laws. Another legal argument is that the punishments are excessive and thus in violation of the Eighth Amendment's prohibition against cruel and unusual punishments.

The lawmakers are still faced with the very grave question: what can we do? If we change the law, *how* do we change it? Do we legalize marijuana entirely? Do we allow people to smoke pot at age sixteen, as the anthropologist Margaret Mead has suggested, or at eighteen as others suggest, or at twenty-one or twenty-five? Do we reduce the penalties, or make marijuana use subject to fines only or to probation only, with eventual dismissal of the charges if the accused behaves himself? And other questions trouble our lawmakers. What will happen if we do change the law? Who can tell us that? What is the alternative to the laws we now have?

In a way, all these arguments have added more heat than light to the legal problem of marijuana. The drug has come to have a greater significance than it deserves. It is seen as the source of "a beautiful, religious, sense-heightening experience" on one hand, and the heraldic device of "anarchistic, war-protesting, college-disrupting, sex-crazy youth" on the other. Caught in-between are the lawmakers, who also live in society, in communities, and who have children—grade school, high school, and college students among them.

Presently Congress is conducting hearings on the drug laws. The Senate Judiciary Committee on 16 December 1969 approved a composite bill submitted by Senator Thomas Dodd of Connecticut and by the Justice Department, which would allow "conditional discharge" to first offenders for possession of certain drugs. The offender would be put on a term of probation and, if the term was completed satisfactorily, the record would be cleared. The bill would also reduce the instances in which judges have to impose mandatory minimum sentences.

The Senate Committee heard arguments with the usual polemics and personal attacks ("Margaret Mead is a dirty old lady," said Governor Claude Kirk of Florida). The Senate passed the bill. Action by the House of Representatives is pending as this book goes to press.

It is highly unlikely that Congress will legalize marijuana, except for its use by researchers. But the proposed bill may clear up horrible confusions in the federal law: to cite an example, the penalties for possession of marijuana exceed those for possession of LSD—an obviously more dangerous drug. A system of penalties more proportionate to the dangers of the various drugs may now reasonably be expected from the Congress. It is significant, however, that the proposed bill was in part presented to the Congress by the Justice Department, which in the early summer of 1969 proposed toughening the penalties, but *now* recommends lessening the penalties for possession of marijuana on the first offense. Yet, Congress, as a body of men elected by the people, more than any other branch of the government is sensitive to changes in the political climate.

If the changes in the drug laws proposed by the Senate Committee are passed, progress will have been made. But whatever Congress does will not change state laws, and they are the ones that count. Federal agencies now rarely, if ever, prosecute for the lesser charge of possession. They seek instead the more serious offenders—the dealers, importers, and sellers—as with Project Intercept, designed to close the Mexican border against the importation of marijuana. The youth who, sitting with his girlfriend in a car on a dark road to smoke a joint that somebody gave him, gets caught by the police will never see federal officials, unless they care to ask him where he got the drug. Federal authorities aren't going to prosecute him. They aren't interested in him and for a variety of reasons, not the least of which is that the federal government does not have the personnel to go after everyone who takes drugs. But the state government is indeed interested in such a youth. State authorities will arrest him for violations of state drug laws and probably charge him with more of these violations than he dreamed existed. For instance, if he lives in Massachusetts, he will be charged not only with possession of marijuana but also with knowingly being in the presence of marijuana, a dangerous and harmful drug, and perhaps with maintaining a public nuisance, transporting a harmful drug, and conspiring to violate the narcotic drug laws. And if his girlfriend is under the age of seventeen, he will be charged with furnishing a drug to a minor and contributing to the delinquency of a minor. The young woman can be charged as well with possession of marijuana and being in the presence of marijuana, a dangerous and harmful drug, and more. The young man can be imprisoned for a total of forty-three years if maximum sentences are given; she for a total of eight and one-half years. Thus, an important point to be remembered is this: the fact that Congress is making changes in federal law may be misleading, because for most drug offenses it is not federal law that matters.

But again, any action taken by Congress will represent progress. Whatever direction the action takes, Congress will have at least indicated its attitude and that will give courage to state legislators, governors, and attorney generals, perhaps encouraging them to follow suit. Also, in its hearings Congress will have assembled a mass of information that the states can use in their decisions to change the drug laws—information that the state legislators often simply do not have. No longer will legislators have to rely on local people whose knowledge may be inadequate or biased. Of course, a note of caution is in order: drug laws will not be changed without hindrance or delay. State legislators, even more than congressional legislators, have to consider their constituency. They are closer to their electorate than congressmen; their districts are smaller. They have less impressive offerings for the electorate than a congressman or senator—a defense contract, a dam, or a reduction in taxes—to compensate for opposing their will. State legislators usually have less money to spend to get re-elected, to explain their positions, and to reason with their electorate. In short, they run even more scared than congressional legislators.

In this regard, even at the federal level, it is interesting to note that the present federal hearings were instigated by the Justice Department, a branch of the presidency. That is, an *appointed* official, the Attorney General of the United States, who heads the Justice Department, authorized this bill to be presented. In contrast, local attorney generals usually are elected and must run for reelection every two to four years. They are far less likely to take political risks, to push controversial legislation.

Nevertheless, at the state level proposals *are* being made by governors, attorney generals, and legislators. After the 3 December 1969 White House Conference of Governors on Drug Abuse, Governor Peterson of New Hampshire, whose daughter saw nothing wrong with smoking pot, suggested that marijuana offenses be classified as misdemeanors rather than felonies. Governor Peterson did not advocate that marijuana be legalized, however, because of insufficient information

163

about its effects. At the conference President Nixon told the governors: "The answer is not more penalties. The answer is information. The answer is understanding." He said that previously he had "thought that the answer was simply enforce the law and that will stop people from the use of drugs. But it is not that." Obviously such a statement had and will have its effect on the governors. When governors receive such messages from both sides—from their children and from the President of the United States—they no doubt begin to reconsider the drug laws of their state. For example, in 1969 the governors of the six New England states recommended a number of revisions in the control of hard drug use (the use of drugs with greater "strength," or potency, than marijuana), although lower penalties was not among them. The governors did not really concern themselves with marijuana, but they did say that most existing laws are unwarranted or "of doubtful constitutionality."

In New York, where the so-called hard drugs create the most serious problems, Governor Nelson Rockefeller praised the approach of the Nixon Administration in a speech to the State Narcotic Addiction Control Commission Conference. A correction official, who coordinates the narcotic programs in California, also told the conference that the distinction between users of marijuana and users of other drugs must be kept in mind. Such a consideration is particularly important in New York, which enacted a "get tough" policy on *all* drug-users in the summer of 1969.

In Massachusetts people at all levels of government have sought changes in the laws that relate to marijuana. The attorney general Robert Quinn has recommended lowering the penalties for possession of marijuana and for knowingly being in its presence. He also has recommended that there be no mandatory minimum sentences for drug offenses, which would mean that a judge could decide the appropriate punishment for each particular case, and has officially sanctioned studies of marijuana in Massachusetts. Two state legislators have filed bills which would reduce the above crimes—possession of marijuana and knowingly being in its presence—to misdemeanors. Other legislators have advocated abolishing these two crimes altogether. At present a special legislative commission, or at least some members of it, are prepared to issue a report which not only recommends abolishing the crime of possession for up to two ounces and the crime of knowingly being in the presence, but also points out the present harshness of other laws in Massachusetts regarding marijuana. This proposed report says:

Under present law, a college student, 21 years old, who shares a marijuana cigarette with his roommate who happens to be 20½, must (not may) be punished by at least 10 years in prison for the technical crime of selling or transferring a narcotic drug.

The commission is not expected to adopt the report entirely, but some lessening of penalties is expected to result; all in all the law will be made more coherent and plausible.

The federal government (through the Justice Department) is preparing a model law to be passed by the states, which will probably be consistent with its present policy as expressed in the proposed bill before Congress: leniency for first offenders charged with possession, particularly of marijuana, and harsh penalties for sellers and dealers. As noted earlier, it was the federal government that suggested the present drug laws in most of the states, by means of a model law— the Uniform Narcotic Drug Act of 1932. So, perhaps it is fitting that the federal government ultimately will encourage the present state laws to be changed.

The *New York Times* reported on 17 August 1969 that

165

some states had changed their drug laws during that year. These changes, which are included in detail in the following chapter, are briefly: New York, Montana, Indiana, and Utah toughened their laws; South Dakota and South Carolina made possession of marijuana on the first offense a misdemeanor; New Mexico made possession of less than one ounce of marijuana a misdemeanor; and Hawaii granted the judge the power to decide if the first offense for marijuana possession is to be a misdemeanor or a felony.

But what is the value to a marijuana user of being charged with a misdemeanor rather than a felony? Misdemeanors are usually punished in county jails and houses of correction—notoriously worse places of confinement than state prisons. As the Eisenhower Commission, appointed by President Johnson to study violence, reported in one of its studies in 1970:

... it should be noted that jails—institutions for detaining accused persons before and during trial and for short misdemeanor sentences—are often the most appalling shame in the criminal justice system. . . . Even more than the prisons, the jails have been indicted as crime breeding institutions.

Even offenders know this. It is not uncommon in Massachusetts for convicted defendants to request a longer state prison term rather than face two and one-half years in a county jail or house of correction. A Massachusetts lawyer, familiar with the state's penal institutions, admits that he would prefer three years in state prison to two years in a county jail or house of correction.

Thus, it does not seem that calling possession or use of marijuana a misdemeanor helps much as far as punishment goes; nor is it really any advantage on a record. The argument is made that, in regard to future employment, educational endeavor, or whatever, a misdemeanor is less harmful

166

on record than a felony. In fact, school administrators and prospective employers want to know *what* crime has been committed, not whether it was a misdemeanor or a felony. If they are vehemently opposed to the use of marijuana or of drugs in general, they will be equally upset whether the offense is called a felony, a misdemeanor, or an infraction.

It is safe to say that most policemen would oppose lowering the penalties for the possession or use of marijuana and certainly would oppose its legalization. The police, who must catch criminals to protect society, as a whole disapprove when the courts demonstrate "softness" toward persons who are guilty of breaking the law. For the most part, the police view the use of drugs, including marijuana, as one more danger to the lives and morality of the public. They often explain our nation's problems as a breakdown in "law and order." They tend to accept substantive laws (such as, burglary shall be punished by a term of three years to longer) yet object to and fight procedural laws (such as, a defendant shall be informed of his rights) with great zeal. Naturally, some policemen see everything that appellate courts and, to a lesser degree, legislatures do solely in relation to themselves as policemen. They evaluate a new decision or law according to whether it will make work easier or more difficult.

To many policemen marijuana is a symbol—a symbol of violent, radical youth and of moral decay. In fact, in most metropolitan areas the police recognize that they simply cannot enforce the drug laws as they stand. Many police departments have given up trying to catch possessors and users and only go after dealers and pushers. And many policemen are becoming better educated about drugs; some realize now that marijuana has been seen somewhat hysterically as the cause of everything bad and evil. Police chiefs and police

167

officers specifically concerned with the drug problem are beginning to understand that inadequate and unenforceable laws are at stake. At certain times, such as at the 1969 Woodstock rock festival in New York, the police may be aware that marijuana is being used publicly, but realize that the dangers of making mass arrests far outweigh the value of the arrests. In our large cities thousands of youths under thirty-five are at least familiar with marijuana. Many, many hundreds use it regularly. The *New York Times* of 23 November 1969 reported a survey which indicated that 50 percent of the youth aged seventeen to nineteen in the entire state of New York are acquainted with someone who has used marijuana.

The police who work on narcotics squads admit that it is absurd for them to try to do the impossible, to catch thousands and thousands of marijuana users. They are far more concerned about other drugs—about amphetamines and barbiturates, which are more available and even can be legally obtained, and about heroin and LSD. The police, in other words, bear the brunt of society's ambiguities; and their general competence must surely be compromised when they cannot enforce laws that would require a virtual army to enforce, backed up by dozens of new, large prisons.

And then, if promotion for a policeman is based on his number of arrests, an unscrupulous policeman wanting to move up the ladder can easily falsify evidence in a marijuana case, especially in those states where possession of even one seed can be cause for conviction. Furthermore, there are instances in which the police are anxious to arrest a particular person, for any number of reasons. As unpleasant as such things are, any prosecutor knows that in a curious way drugs can advance corruption in the police force. When a law no longer commands the respect of a significant minority and indeed is considered harsh and unfair by a larger minority, the police will not be able to enforce that law and may selectively use it for devious purposes, thereby increasing rather than reducing a society's injustice.

Diverse attitudes toward the marijuana laws can be found among police officers, as illustrated by the following breakdown of student attitudes within a single criminology class in Massachusetts. One question on the final exam concerned proposed changes in the penalties for the crimes of possession of marijuana and of knowingly being in its presence. Many of the fifty-four policemen taking the exam thought that the standing penalties in Massachusetts (up to three and one-half years for possession and up to five years for knowingly being in the presence of marijuana) were appropriate. Many students, however, thought that the penalties should be reversed; that is, up to five years for possession and up to three and one-half years for knowingly being in the presence of marijuana. A substantial number thought that the crime "knowingly being in the presence of marijuana" ought to be abolished. One student said, "You don't arrest a baseball player, even though he knows that there is gambling going on in the grandstand." A few students wanted to raise both penalties, and a few wanted to lower them. Most believed that high penalties produced a deterrent effect and that the use of marijuana leads to the use of stronger drugs like LSD, speed, and heroin. Yet almost all indicated that the law and its institutions are incapable of solving the marijuana problem; they thought the only possible solution would come from education—in the home, in the schools (beginning with grade school), on television, and in the press. Other students suggested that young people

169

be better informed of the dangers of drug abuse through graphic movies, visits to drug treatment centers, or discussions with ex-addicts.

Although the exam question dealt specifically with marijuana, the policemen's answers, in many instances, related to drugs in general. Some students denied that alcohol was a drug, but almost all saw no merit whatsoever to the proposition that because alcohol, a drug, is legalized or regulated, then marijuana, a drug of roughly similar effect, also should be legalized and regulated. Again and again the answers in essence asked, "Who needs another alcohol?"

The policemen, most of whom were patrolmen (the lowest rank in the police force) deplored the lack of specific knowledge about marijuana and noted frequent contradictions among so-called experts, even when from the same source, such as the government. Most thought, however, that this very lack of specific knowledge is reason enough to keep the present laws until more knowledge is gained.

These criminology students had in no way been prepared for this question on their exam. The subject matter was not a part of the curriculum, and the policemen were assured that there were no right or wrong answers and that grades would be based on the reasoning used rather than the opinions expressed. About one-half of the policemen lived in a city of about 185,000 people and the rest, in smaller cities and towns. All agreed that there was a problem of marijuana and youth.

Lawyers are too often silent when it comes to social causes. Men like Ralph Nader are few indeed, and organizations like the American Civil Liberties Union are not among the most powerful in their influence on lawyers. Thus, while the American Medical Association has had a lot to say about marijuana, the American Bar Association has not yet addressed itself to the problems of marijuana and other drugs, as far as we know. One lawyer who has spoken and written at length on the subject of marijuana is Joseph Oteri, whose position is made clear in an article published in April 1968:

It is my personal feeling that marijuana is no more harmful than alcohol and that American citizens should be free to choose between the two; provided, however, that:

1. There be an emergency appropriation by the Congress of the United States to subsidize a crash study of the short and long term effects of marijuana on the users. If marijuana is found to be a mild hallucinogenic drug with a relatively minor capacity for abuse then,

2. The legislature should enact a system of regulation similar to that which controls the distribution of alcohol with special emphasis on quality control, and age of purchasers.

3. Criminal penalties should remain for those who sell the drug to minors or deal in illicit drugs; i.e., bootleggers.

Until this millennium is arrived at, I would strongly urge that the treatment of persons arrested for possession of small amounts of marijuana or for being present where marijuana is kept illegally, be handled on the basis of a medical and social problem. This can be done within the existing court structure by referring the arrested person to a psychiatrist, having the probation officers work with him and his family and eventually, at the expired period of time during which the person demonstrates his social value, the charges be dismissed, thus preventing what I consider to be the greatest harm which can befall a person; i.e., a criminal record for a narcotic violation.

In conclusion, it should be realized that pot is the most harmful drug in the world because it is illegal and its use or possession carries with it Draconian penalties. Many young lives are ruined because of a kid's desire to experiment with "grass." Those of us who are aware of the problem are doing all we can to change what we consider to be bad laws, but unless and until they are changed, they are the law of the land and will be enforced by the police and the courts, and the young person who

171

is willing to risk all the opportunities that are available to him in this country for the pleasure of smoking a marijuana cigarette should be pitied rather than prosecuted.

On 6 December 1969 the *New York Times* reported that two district attorneys in New York, Thomas J. Mackell of Queens and Burton B. Roberts of the Bronx, recommended lowering the penalties for possession of varying amounts of marijuana. District Attorney Mackell said that the present New York laws are not only "absurd and ridiculous" in themselves but unequal in relation to penalties for other more dangerous drugs, such as barbiturates and amphetamines. No doubt other prosecutors agree, but are silent. At present, all that they can do—indeed they do so all the time—is recommend probation or continuances with eventual dismissal after a stated period of time—contingent on the good conduct of the accused. The legal profession, like any other, will change with the change of generations, and some of our drug laws, among others, will eventually be changed too. A poll at Columbia Law School reported by the *New York Times* showed that: 69 percent of the 491 law students polled admitted to smoking marijuana at least once; 53 percent said they used it once or twice a month; 97 percent said they thought the law should be liberalized; and 96 percent said that persons arrested for marijuana use should not be refused admittance to the bar. (At the present time an arrest for possession of marijuana excludes a person from practice as a lawyer.)

As for judges, they talk about cases, not causes. Unless faced with an actual case requiring clarification, they usually do not discuss pertinent issues in hypothetical situations, in court or out. Some judges have spoken out, however, apart from the judicial opinions they have handed down. In a speech delivered in England in November 1969, David L. Bazelon, Chief Judge of the United States Court of Appeals for the

District of Columbia, questioned the very idea of punishing drug offenders; questioned the statistics connecting drug use and dangerous crimes, like burglary and robbery; questioned civil commitment—the practice of sending the accused to a drug treatment center rather than to jail; and pointed out that treatment centers often are in no better shape than prisons:

If we agree to confine—by civil commitment or criminal process—only those drug users who are dangerous to others, we are left with the vast numbers of drug users who harm only themselves. For these people, the criminal laws against drug use interfere with essential private conduct. Like laws against suicide, or laws against riding a motorcycle without a helmet, they limit one man's liberty without protecting anyone else. Putting a man in jail is a rather primitive way of protecting him.

The speech ends with this series of assertions:

Our scientific knowledge about drugs was slim when we enacted our present drug laws, and it is not much more extensive now. The difference is that now we are beginning to recognize how little we know—and that is the first step toward finding out. We have arrived at that terrible period known as meanwhile, when we know enough to raise doubts but not enough to resolve them.

Any step we take will amount to little more than shooting in the dark. The basic values of our culture demand that we err on the side of individual liberty. But until we have done a better job of mapping out the terrain, there is always a chance that the individual will fall. When he does, we should reach out to him not with a club but a helping hand.

Judge Charles J. Wyzanski, the Chief of the United States District Court of Massachusetts, which sits in Boston, has said:

. . . Many of the arguments that are presented against marijuana are specious. It is, of course, absurd to argue that because

173

most users of heroin first used marijuana, marijuana is proven to be a usual preliminary step to heroin addiction. One might as well say that because most users of heroin once imbibed milk, milk leads to heroin addiction. The true inquiry is what percentage of marijuana users become heroin addicts, and as to that we seem to have no reliable information.

Undoubtedly for those who use marijuana so frequently and so excessively as to become social derelicts, society pays a large cost. In the first place, these unfortunates use either private or public resources for their medical and social care. In the second place, and of greater consequence, our relatively limited medical, hospital, and welfare personnel and facilities used for those victims of marijuana are unavailable for others whose illness or poverty is more deserving of our compassion. The social balance sheet bears charges which ought not to be in the reckoning.

From the foregoing facts, it does appear that the marijuana problem is of social, and not merely of private, consequence. J. S. Mill to the contrary notwithstanding, there is no such thing as a vice which is purely private in its total aspect. He who overindulges in any way with respect to drugs, with respect to food, with respect to liquor, with respect to sensuality, alters the lives of others than himself and his private associates. He is unavailable for civic obligation which rests upon him. He bears a responsibility for the unavailability of social and medical services gravely needed by others.

Yet against the impressive considerations just stated, one must weigh—and in my opinion weigh more heavily—the social costs of trying to limit by law private indulgence in vice . . .

In the end, liberty tends to be sacrificed for the supposedly greater advantage of health, safety, and morals. To some, including myself, the sacrifice is inconsistent with our ultimate political beliefs.

For these reasons, it would seem to me highly desirable if the legislative authorities, national and local, were to revise the present laws with respect to marijuana with their Draconian penalties . . .

What seems to me required is that, acting on their own initiative, leaders of undergraduate opinion and leaders of the same age, but not from academic cloisters, should carefully consider their own forums and through their own organizations, and through specially created mediums of expression and forms of association, a policy and a plan for its execution. [The solution to the marijuana problem.]

A more candid view was given by Judge Elijah Adlow of the Boston Municipal Court, the Lower Level Trial Court for Boston which tries all those accused of committing state crimes in the city. The judge sees every kind of criminal and hears descriptions of every kind of crime. In an interview reported in *Sui Juris,* the newspaper of the Boston College Law School, he is quoted as follows:

Marijuana offers nothing to anybody. It is a pure illusion. There is nothing more satisfying than good, clear, fresh air—living a normal life. These kids have long lives if they don't abuse them . . . I think the immediate obligation of society is to curb the traffic of drugs, and it has to be done without fear or favor. In the society in which we live, anything which deprives a man of his faculties, that impairs his judgment, that conduces to his eventual invalidism is a public matter.

The article points out, however, that Judge Adlow feels that the offender to be jailed is the pusher rather than the user. For the user he recommends a "rehabilitative" attitude.

The best indication of what trial judges think is still their sentences. Generally, across the nation, the emphasis has changed from punishment of drug users to punishment of sellers and dealers. Many judges have changed their minds, just as President Nixon did.

In one respect judges have a little less pressure on their decisions than lawmakers. They often are appointed and can become their own men—if they want to. True, some are elected, which creates political problems, but the problems are not as grave as those facing legislators, governors, and attorney generals. Judges often run unopposed or are endorsed by all political parties, and their terms are longer than those of elected officials. But judges have serious frustrations, however well protected their positions are. The laws are there—of somebody else's making—and often enough give a judge little or no leeway. For instance, a judge might be required to hand down a penalty of twenty-five years in prison to a youth found guilty of furnishing marijuana to a minor. Such a penalty applies whether or not the guilty party has ever been in trouble before, whether or not what he furnished was a puff of one joint; whether or not he was a minor himself or just over the age of minority by a few days; whether or not he had up until then been a boy scout, an altar boy, the captain of the football team, president of his high school class, and editor of the school paper; and whether or not he is the sole support of his mother whose husband died in Korea or Vietnam. The judge has to, if the boy is found guilty, send him to jail for the mandatory term.

Of course, when the law is not so strict, when there is no mandatory penalty, the judge can, if he wants to, impose the minimum penalty or less. He can put the offender on probation or continue the case for later dismissal and clearance of the record. But judges, too, are sensitive to public pressure, particularly in small communities but also in large ones. There is no doubt that the United States Supreme Court, whose constituency is the entire nation, was watching the 1968 national election results even before Chief Justice Earl Warren's resignation. Judges and courts change. In 1969 when the Supreme Court (then called the Warren Court) threw out convictions against Dr. Timothy Leary, the famous proponent of LSD, relating to the importation of marijuana, the Court said that the Marijuana Tax Stamp Act was unconstitutional. (If one wanted marijuana, one had to pay a tax and get a stamp, but nobody was to be given a stamp because supposedly there is no legitimate use for marijuana.) The Court held that the act required a person to incriminate himself contrary to the Fifth Amendment. The government could and would report the possession of marijuana to the local state government. In 1970 the Supreme Court (called the Burger Court) held that this requirement is unconstitutional only when applied to purchasers and importers; that it is permissible to apply it to peddlers and sellers.

One Massachusetts judge recently commented informally that he wished the police would stop bringing before him minors who carried liquor in cars and youths who smoked marijuana. He preferred the police to pay attention to "more serious crimes." But this judge is particularly liberal and widely traveled; his judicial attitude is probably the exception rather than the rule. In Massachusetts most judges are lenient with first offenders charged with possession of marijuana or knowingly being in its presence. But that is because they are allowed to be (not all state laws would let them) and because the climate of opinion in the state encourages such a posture. States, like individual judges, vary in such attitudes.

One theory of jurisprudence has it that the dispensation of justice on any given day is a matter of what the judge had for breakfast. Obviously, judges can be arbitrary, gratuitous, and unpredictable—even the best of them—and particularly so when the case before them is not cut-and-dried. Sometimes judges suddenly decide to make an example of a guilty party. Such seems to have been the case with Frank P. La Varre, the almost definitive "all-American boy"—track star, fine student—who was convicted in Virginia for possess-

177

ing over twenty-five grains of marijuana. *Life* magazine covered the story in its 31 October 1969 issue on marijuana. Because Mr. La Varre refused to turn informer, the judge jumped his bail three times from $5,000 to $50,000; the judge sentenced him to twenty-five years in prison with five years suspended for good behavior. La Varre's sentence has since been commuted by the governor; however, everyone is not so fortunate as to have *Life* as an advocate. (The magazine noted that La Varre read all he could about marijuana, but then adds, "He forgot to read about the drug laws.")

The point then is not what judges in a particular area usually do, but what they *can* do and what *can* be done that is subject to attack on appeal—if an appeal can be afforded. The sentence given by a judge is rarely overturned if it is within the limits of the stated penalty for the law. The Eighth Amendment to the Constitution forbids "cruel and unusual punishments," but it is one of the amendments still to be clarified with regard to many different criminal laws.

Judges are, no doubt, as confused about marijuana as the public. They don't know what steps should be taken, but apparently most of them do not think the laws against marijuana should be repealed entirely (and that includes the liberal judge mentioned earlier, who was more bored with the problem than anything else). However, marijuana is probably getting the benefit of the doubt more and more often in less serious cases, such as possession in small amounts.

In 1968 a serious legal attack took place on the validity of the scientific assumptions behind the marijuana laws. This case is worth noting because the "expert" evidence was more extensive than any previously brought together and because for the first time an attack was made on the validity of the laws themselves rather than on the penalties or the enforce-

178

ment of drug laws. The case, called the *Leis and Weiss* case, was presided over by Chief Justice G. Joseph Tauro of the Massachusetts Superior Court. A very able trial lawyer, James D. St. Clair, was made a special assistant district attorney in order to handle the case. (St. Clair was an assistant to Joseph Welch in the Senator Joseph McCarthy Hearings.) The defense was argued by Joseph Oteri, who in the *Village Voice* of 20 November, 1969 was called the "Boston attorney who has become widely known as a pot defender." The case, in fact remarkably free of emotion, was an example of the legal process at its best.

The facts, which are fairly simple, were not really in dispute. Leis and Weiss, two young men, went to Boston's Logan Airport with a claim check to pick up a trunk. They were met by narcotics agents, who found the trunk to contain fifty pounds of sand and five pounds of marijuana. As in many cases today and in drug cases especially, the important issues were presented and resolved in a pre-trial hearing, in this instance on a motion to dismiss the case. (That is, before the trial was held to determine whether Leis and Weiss were guilty of their charges—possessing marijuana, conspiracy to violate the narcotic drug law, and possessing marijuana with intent to sell—a hearing was held in front of the judge to determine if the laws were even constitutional. If it had been determined that they were not constitutional, then obviously there would have been no trial.)

The defense claimed that marijuana is not a narcotic; that it is not a harmful drug or that if it is, so are other things that aren't forbidden, such as alcohol and nicotine; that the classification of marijuana as a narcotic is arbitrary and without scientific basis, and thus unconstitutional; that the marijuana punishments are "cruel and unusual"; and that the pur-

179

suit of pleasure through marijuana is a right allowed by, even though not mentioned in, the Constitution. (The rights to read, teach, or raise a family are not specifically mentioned in the Constitution, but nobody denies that these rights exist.)

The prosecution argued that marijuana is a harmful drug, that it creates a "psychological dependence," and that there is no such right to pleasure as outlined by the defense. Eighteen witnesses were called—medical doctors, psychologists, sociologists, a botanist, pharmacologists, a theologian, a philosopher, and other "experts" from as far away as Greece and India.

The judge wrote a ruling, based on this testimony, that gave his reasons for denying the motion to dismiss. Three premises, each of which can be traced to the "expert" testimony, ran through the ruling. The first premise was that marijuana is a psychologically dependent drug (that is, users become *psychologically,* as opposed to *physically,* dependent on it); in that sense marijuana is not arbitrarily classified with heroin and other drugs as a narcotic. The second premise was that the users of marijuana are "emotionally unstable" or "marginally stable" people. The judge says, ". . . there is widespread emotional instability among the users of marijuana." He goes on to state that "the ordinary user of marijuana is quite likely to be a marginally adjusted person who turns to the drug to avoid confrontation with and resolution of his problems." The third premise was that marijuana is not used in the same way as alcohol: marijuana is used as an intoxicant in an all-or-nothing fashion, while alcohol is used as a relaxant. The various effects of alcohol—becoming first relaxed, mellow, and then progressively drunker—are judged either not possible or irrelevant in the case of marijuana and its users. The chief justice says, "the drug, as it is commonly used, has as its primary and, as far as I can ascertain, its only purpose the induction of a state of intoxication or euphoria." Granted these premises (which are discussed in other parts of this book), the result of the case is not any great surprise.

The judge and the prosecution considered the basic issue of the case to be whether marijuana is a harmful or dangerous drug and thus properly classified by the law as a narcotic. It is interesting to note that the judge says, ". . . the term *narcotic*, as currently used is a legal term with no precise, clinical meaning and is employed to describe a varied assortment of harmful and dangerous drugs." The defense, in contrast, considered the basic issue to be whether the "pursuit of happiness" through marijuana is a fundamental right—marijuana being as equally valid a route as alcohol, which is not prohibited but regulated.

Both sides deplored the lack of good research on the subject, both at the time of the trial and at the time of the passing of the laws. As Chief Justice Tauro said, ". . . There was some reference to the legislative history [research on which the laws are based] of our narcotic drug laws or rather, more properly to the lack of any such complete history." And everybody agreed that the legislature should look closely at the standing penalties, particularly regarding possession. Indeed, St. Clair, the prosecutor in the case, noted:

This is not to say, however, that consideration should not now be given to reappraisal of the existing laws and especially the penalties called for. It is difficult for example to justify the 5 year mandatory offense under Federal law for transferring marijuana. While this statute was undoubtedly aimed at the persons engaged in large scale commercial traffic in marijuana, its breadth covers the student who hands a marijuana cigarette to another or divides his small supply with a friend. The imposition under Massachusetts law of a larger penalty for being

181

present where marijuana is illegally kept than for actually possessing it is also hard to justify.

Adjustments can and should be made to correct such excesses and inconsistencies. *If they are corrected much of the disrespect for the drug laws now existing among many of the youth of the country may disappear.* If at the same time the other interested professions concentrate on research programs to evaluate the effects of the use of marijuana and the other psychoactive drugs and the law is then made consistent with those results, a solid basis will be established to recommend such laws to the youth who predictably will be inclined to afford such laws far more respect [italics ours].

After the ruling was made by the Chief Justice of the Superior Court, the defense appealed the decision to the Massachusetts Supreme Judicial Court (the highest state court), where it was affirmed. The Court added, "The Defendants have no right, fundamental or otherwise, to become intoxicated by means of the smoking of marijuana." The Supreme Judicial Court generally adopted Chief Justice Tauro's opinion, but it said that *enough,* rather than *all,* users are marginally stable and that marijuana leads *some,* rather than *many,* people to worse things —and presumably *some* is quite enough. The court further said, in effect, that because no one knows how marijuana really works —and because we know what alcohol does and can determine its effects, but we cannot do so with marijuana—it is better to leave the prohibition on the books.

Although it changed no law at all, the *Leis and Weiss* case served useful purposes. First, the validity of the laws regarding marijuana at last was examined—the law's logical, scientific, and commonsensical validity. And the examination and analysis were done in the courts, where political pressures were kept at a certain distance. Second, suggestions were made

182

with respect to changes in the penalties—suggestions which could encourage lawmakers to reexamine the statutes. Had this hearing not been held, the attorney general of Massachusetts in November 1969 would probably not have allowed marijuana research to be officially conducted—an important step in bringing reason to bear on the whole issue. Third, the hearing provided a good deal of information for judges in the other trial courts, so that they could reexamine their own view of the laws and rid themselves of what the defense called "the myths and misrepresentations which have been promulgated since at least the mid-1930's and which have cast marijuana as a villain and an assassin." Because it was conducted by Chief Justice Tauro, the chief trial judge in the state, the hearing encouraged rational discussion among judges of lesser rank and lawyers. And fourth, a precedent was set for reexamination of the laws once better and more reliable evidence has been gathered.

Joseph Oteri has since represented a person arrested for possession of marijuana in his own home in Florida. Mr. Oteri moved to dismiss, as in the *Leis and Weiss* case, and presented a transcript of the evidence taken at the *Leis and Weiss* hearing along with further medical evidence. Again, the motion was denied by both the Trial Court and the Appeals Court, and from such denial the case has been appealed to the United States Supreme Court where it now awaits action.

The usual case involving a violation of the marijuana laws is often, in fact, two separate cases, just as the *Leis and Weiss* case was. There is usually in such cases a preliminary hearing on motions (but not usually a motion to dismiss that asserts the laws are invalid). Since the case of *Mapp* v. *Ohio*

183

was decided by the Warren Court, the practice of criminal law has had a new aspect. Now, before the trial of every case in which there has been "anything in the nature of a search" performed by the police, the court at the request of the accused looks at the circumstances surrounding the search. If it finds that the search did not meet the standards set by the Fourth Amendment to the Constitution, the court will not allow the prosecution to present any evidence gained directly or indirectly as a result of that search.

In the now famous *Miranda* case (*Miranda* v. *Arizona*) the same United States Supreme Court later decided there were certain things that an accused must be told and must understand before he could be questioned. If he is not told or does not understand each of these things, any evidence gained as a result of questions answered by the defendant can be thrown out. Because they are based on the Constitution, these two rulings apply to all the states. It is essential that every citizen know about his rights under the *Mapp* v. *Ohio* case and the *Miranda* case, because these rights are now the most important issues in most criminal cases and, indeed, most likely in all drug cases.

Therefore, a person accused of violating a drug law should take this advice, which is deceptively simple and frequently ignored: get the best criminal lawyer possible. Remember that the law looks upon a guilty party as a criminal. Although drug laws may eventually be changed, at present all drug offenses are crimes. The accused person should also be aware of his rights as a citizen. The Fourth Amendment reads:

The right of the people to be secure in their persons, houses, papers, and effects, against unreasonable searches and seizures, shall not be violated, and no warrants shall issue, but upon probable cause, supported by Oath or affirmation, and particularly

184

describing the place to be searched; and the persons or things to be seized.

The Fourth Amendment, as interpreted by the courts, means that the police cannot search a person's home or "effects"—his car, his suitcases—or his "person" without a warrant based on probable cause supported by oath *or* unless the search is incidental to an arrest based on probable cause. A subrule of the interpretation holds that if the police have time to get a warrant, they must do so. Most lower courts tend to be less rigid about the subrule than higher courts. Because for a number of reasons policemen do not like to prepare affidavits and apply for warrants, searches of people often take place "incidental" to arrests without warrants. A search warrant allows the police to search anything in the area described by the warrant. For example, if the warrant directs a search of an apartment, the police can search the apartment but not the entire apartment house. Assuming that they make a valid arrest in an apartment without a warrant, the police probably are not permitted even to search the entire apartment. So, from the point of view of the police, the search warrant allows them to search more area, while the search without a warrant allows them to search without the formalities but in a more limited space.

The police can seize, or take with them, certain limited types of things. They can take contraband, which marijuana is because nobody has any right to it; they can take stolen property; and, under a recent ruling, they can take evidence. Therefore, if they make a raid in an apartment and find marijuana, the police can take it and do not have to return it. If they find property which they know is stolen, such as an identifiable television set, they can seize that, too. And they can take all sorts of paraphernalia that is in itself not illegal—such as

185

pipes, cigarette papers, and incense—but may help support their case. The paraphernalia would probably have to be returned regardless of the verdict, but the marijuana and the TV, if proved to be stolen, would not.

There are certain other important rules regarding a search. If the police make a search without a warrant because they have probable cause to believe that some type of illegal activity is going on, and they then find such activity indeed going on in addition to another illegal activity, they are limited in the extent to which they can attempt to curb the second type of activity. For example, the police, believing that a given man is a receiver of stolen television sets, obtain a warrant and search the man's apartment for the stolen sets, whose serial numbers and descriptions they have. Perhaps they find the sets, but they cannot then search a jewelry box, four inches by six inches, because it is less than likely that a stolen television set would be hidden there. If the police do so anyway and find marijuana, in most cases the marijuana cannot be used against the man in a prosecution for violation of the drug laws, because the law says the police have gone "beyond the scope of their probable cause."

On the other hand, if the police search a man's apartment for stolen television sets and incidentally see on the kitchen table a pile of a "green herblike substance" (a favorite phrase the police use to describe marijuana) which they in their knowledge and experience believe to be marijuana, the substance can be seized. This is true because the substance is contraband, which no one has a right to, and because as a drug the substance is the "subject," so to speak, of a crime— possession of marijuana—that is being committed in the presence of law officers.

Ideally then, when on a search the police must have a good

186

idea what they are looking for and where they might find it. This information must be written on the affidavit required to obtain a warrant; what the police can seize and where they can find it also must be written on the warrant itself. If a search without a warrant is questioned, the police must be able to tell what knowledge justified the search. In other words, after the search has taken place, they have to be able to establish what they knew before the search that allowed them to do what they did. The possible abuses this kind of hindsight, this Monday morning quarterbacking, lends itself to should be apparent.

With or without a warrant, a policeman can *say* that he saw marijuana in an openly visible place. In the above example the police saw a "green herblike substance" on the kitchen table while looking for something else. But suppose the "herbs" had been discovered in a drawer or in a jewelry box; nevertheless the police could *say* that they found them on the table. There is really nothing to prevent them from lying about where they found the marijuana and indeed from getting away with the lie—except their own honesty and integrity. The only person to dispute the police is the accused, who wouldn't advance the impression he is trying to make by testifying that "the grass was in a box." The accused would thereby be admitting that he had possessed the drug—that indeed he had committed a crime. In any case, who is the court in all likelihood going to believe? There is almost an unwritten presumption in the minds of many judges that policemen are to be believed—period.

In another common occurrence, the police stop a certain car for some minor reason—a taillight doesn't work or a driver is speeding. If a hidden drug, say marijuana, is discovered in the stopped car, the police can claim that they saw it on the seat of the car, on the floor, falling from the driver's pocket as he got out of the car, or in the glove compartment when the driver was looking for his registration. Or the police can ask the driver to open his trunk under the false pretense that they want to check the taillight wiring—and claim to have found marijuana there. The police can also, upon smelling marijuana in a stopped car, ask the driver if they may search the car.

Surely thousands of American youths must realize what can happen to them if they risk breaking the law. Situations like those described above are not covered by the search regulations set forth in the Fourth Amendment. A search has not taken place when a policeman spots something in open view from outside a car. And any illegal substance can be seized if the policeman has enough experience, training, or knowledge to be able to tell with substantial certainty what the substance is. Moreover, the police know what is and what is not covered by the Fourth Amendment. It is no secret that the police upon occasion stop certain cars for minor reasons because, in fact, the people inside look "suspicious": they are "wild-looking" or they are "hippies." The police have preconceived ideas about the physical appearance of drug users, and they know that they can find a reason to stop almost any car on the road.

So, apart from their own honesty and morality, there is nothing really to prevent the police from saying that they have seen marijuana in open view, when in fact they have conducted a search in violation of the Fourth Amendment. And again, the only person who can refute the police under such circumstances is the defendant, who is in the awkward position of saying, "Yes, I was breaking the law—but I wasn't caught in a legal way." Whether a judge is going to be impressed by such testimony is a matter of his own personality and philosophy. In most instances, no doubt, the judge will go along with the police and remain uninfluenced by the defendant's plea that somehow one thing has led to another so that he is now charged not with speeding, but with possessing marijuana.

Another kind of search that is allowed by the Fourth Amendment is called a "consent search." For example, a man drives down Main Street in his car with one light out. A policeman stops him and approaches the car. The driver rolls down his window and asks, "What's the matter?" The policeman answers, "Your right taillight is out." The driver says, "I didn't know." The policeman says, "Get out and look if you don't believe me." When the driver gets out, the policeman observes that he has long hair and is wearing twenty-inch bellbottoms and a flowery T-shirt dyed purple. The officer says, "I smell grass and you put something under the seat as I came over. May I search this car?" The driver may know that he doesn't have to let the policeman search the car, but even if he doesn't, the policeman must inform him that he may refuse to consent. But the driver may assume that what he hid will never be found or that if he refuses, the policeman will hold him anyway until a warrant to search the car is obtained. So, the driver tells the policeman, "Go ahead." The policeman searches and let us assume that he does find marijuana. He then arrests the driver for a violation of the law of the road—operating a car with a defective taillight—to establish his initial reason for stopping the car. Then he charges the driver with possession of marijuana, or with possession with intent to sell if more than a small amount is found, or maybe even with illegally transporting the drug. The driver calls a lawyer, gets out on bail, and is brought to trial.

Prior to the actual trial, the defense lawyer files a motion to suppress the introduction of the marijuana as evidence on the ground that the car was illegally searched and the marijuana illegally seized. He more specifically states the facts of the case and argues that the driver did not consent to "waive his constitutional right" to be free from a search based on less than "probable cause." Although hopefully the nature of the consent is quite closely examined, the chances are that the court will find that the driver did consent to the search and therefore has no reason, or "no standing," to object.

Now, suppose the driver had said, "No, you cannot search my car." And suppose the officer had anyway and decided, for reasons best known to himself, to testify that the driver consented to the search. Who is going to be believed? And who is going to be believed especially if the policeman finds five or six pounds or five or six kilos (rather a lot) of marijuana? The judge will realize that he has a big case before him and that he will be heavily criticized unless he sustains the police—United States Constitution or no Constitution. Perhaps he has never made a distinction between marijuana and heroin, and he has read the local state law that classifies them together as "narcotics." The judge will not be inclined to give the driver much credence, particularly since he did actually possess marijuana.

Recently the Supreme Court, in the course of deciding a California case, discussed at length the laws that cover "consent searches." The previous interpretation was that if the person in possession of the given premises consented to a search that uncovered evidence to be used against a second party, then the second party could not object. For example, a man lives or is staying at his girlfriend's house or apartment, which she owns or possesses. The police observe a suspicious man walking in and out of the house and, when he has left, they approach the house and ring the bell. The woman answers the door and the police say, "We've seen a suspicious-looking man going in and out of this house. May we search it?" The woman may not think that her friend would ever do anything wrong or that he would leave marijuana in her place, or she may be intimidated by the idea of the police; in any event, she agrees and the police find and seize ten ounces of marijuana.

Until recently the accused man had "no standing" to object to that search and seizure. It was interpreted that *his* right to be secure in *his* house was not violated, because this house belonged to the girl. Now the courts would rule that the man can object and that his girlfriend's consent should not affect him. Because he is affected by the search, he can protest and move to suppress the evidence, which must then be thrown out. This interpretation is now applicable to short- and long-term guests in apartments and hotels, and even to people who have keys to the home of another person, arrive without notice, and stay there without the other person's knowledge.

Whether such an interpretation applies to parents and their own children, who live with them, has not been decided yet. But the Supreme Court's position has been applied to a situation in which a boy and his friend were staying with the boy's grandmother. The grandmother consented to a search of her house, which did uncover evidence, and the evidence was suppressed in court.

The *Miranda* case, of recent fame, clarified a citizen's right upon arrest to be informed of his constitutional rights in a way he can understand. If an accused person is not so informed, any incriminating statements he makes cannot be used against him. These rights, like those that regulate searches, are provided by the Constitution and so apply to all proceedings, whether in a court or not, in all of the states and territories.

If in a pre-trial hearing the judge finds that the rights of the accused have been violated, then the results, direct or indirect, of that violation cannot be used by the state against the accused in the criminal trial to follow.

To be explicit, the rights clarified by the *Miranda* case are:

1. You have a right to remain silent.
2. Anything you say can and probably will be used against you in court.
3. You have a right to a lawyer now and a right to a lawyer at any time during the interrogation.
4. If you cannot afford a lawyer, one will be provided for you.
5. You have a right to make a telephone call to consult anyone —lawyer, doctor, or family. (This right, although not explicitly set forth by the *Miranda* case, is incidental to exercising the other rights.)

And in order to get a waiver of these rights, a policeman must ask:

1. Do you understand what I have said?
2. Understanding what I said, do you waive your rights?

Not only must the accused understand what is said to him but the police must be able to show in court that he was capable of understanding and indeed did understand. Whether an intoxicated person can understand his rights is an undecided question. Some courts have decided that a person high on marijuana or another drug cannot understand and therefore cannot effectively waive his rights.

After showing that the accused did understand, the state must show that he effectively waived his rights. The question of his capability to do so again arises. Silence alone is not a waiver, nor is a blank stare. A waiver is not effective if the accused says nothing about waiving his rights, but answers a question such as, "Where did you get the grass?" His answer cannot be used as evidence against him unless he has explicitly said or done something to unquestionably indicate that he has waived his rights.

In a recent decision, which essentially restated the *Miranda* case, the United States Supreme Court held that there are *no* exceptions—that *everyone* must be informed of his rights. The decision implied that if a chief justice of the Supreme Court were arrested, even *he* would have to be informed of his rights and effectively waive them before anything he said could serve as evidence against him.

Since it must be given in every case, most policemen now either know the "Miranda warning" by heart or carry cards from which to read it. But because they sometimes make mistakes, a lawyer should be very careful to find out exactly what the police did and said during an arrest. Certain negative attitudes toward the Miranda decision linger from the great resistance it originally met. When testifying that an accused was informed of his rights, a policeman often will add something like this: "I told him he could use the phone *at his own expense*." The phrase *at his own expense* indicates the policeman's unwillingness to recognize a constitutional right, which belongs even to a pauper.

Failure to inform an arrested person of his rights or an illegal search and seizure does not necessarily result in a dismissal of the charges. If in a pre-trial hearing he finds that either has occurred, the judge orders "suppression of the evidence 'obtained as a result of' the illegal search" or "the failure to inform." If the only evidence in the case is a confession obtained without informing the defendant of his rights, then that confession cannot be presented at the trial and the accused will

193

have to be found "not guilty." Thus the hearing determines what evidence will be presented in the trial.

If the police raid an apartment solely because they see two youths with beards entering, the chances are that the search would be declared an illegal one. If they find marijuana while in the apartment, it cannot be used as evidence against the youths in a trial for "possession" or for any other charge. Even evidence not directly connected to the violation of rights must be suppressed. For example, a man, who has a beard and looks like a hippie, is stopped for speeding. The police for no reason other than his appearance search the man and his car, finding nothing but a note in his pocket: "Maryjane $10 at 473 Main Street between six and midnight every night but Thursday." The police, suspecting that "Maryjane" is a code name for or a translation of marijuana, notify the narcotics squad, which puts the building at 473 Main Street under surveillance. They observe enough activity to justify a warrant and a subsequent raid, during which marijuana is indeed found. Despite the search warrant, the court would or should suppress the evidence because the initial search of the driver was in violation of his rights under the Fourth Amendment. Any evidence obtained as the indirect result of an illegal search is also unusable.

In an example of "the failure to inform," a man, stopped for speeding, is questioned extensively in the police cruiser although he is never officially put under arrest. Because he is not free to leave, the courts would describe his situation as "custodial." During the questioning he is asked, "Who sells you your grass?" He answers, "I grow it myself." The police search his house and find ten healthy female marijuana plants in addition to a list of names and addresses with dates, times, and amounts after them. One entry—"Mary Moose, 17 Spring Street, 10:30, 17 November 1969, $20"—is for that very night, about one-half an hour before the arrest. The police search 17 Spring Street and find an ounce of marijuana. They charge the driver with possession of marijuana, possession with intent to sell, growing marijuana, and selling marijuana, using the list of information and the seized ounce of marijuana as evidence. But the evidence must be suppressed because the initial questioning was illegal: the man had not been informed of his rights. Could the police, however, use the ounce of marijuana as evidence against Mary Moose of 17 Spring Street on a charge of possession? It would seem that they could, unless some aspect of the search of her house could be proved illegal. It was the driver whose rights had been violated.

The above examples only begin to suggest the variety of such illegal proceedings that have appeared before the courts. There are no specific guidelines that all accused persons might follow, because legal decisions depend on the particular facts and circumstances of each case. Even the Supreme Court of the United States does not decide hypothetical cases.

Many marijuana cases are heard in federal or state district courts, municipal courts, or lower trial courts and tried without a jury. There is frequently a right of appeal to a higher trial court, with or without a jury, but in some cases the appeals go directly to the highest court of the state, where the propriety of the conduct of the trial is evaluated. (Each state has its own system of courts and methods of appeal, resulting in great diversity.) In any event, each step involves cost, making the entire appeal quite an expensive matter. Lawyers cost money; good lawyers cost more money, and the best lawyers cost a lot of money. The lawyer usually charges more for a second trial and much more for an appeal to the highest state court, usually called the state supreme court or the court of appeals. Thousands of appeals are never made because the

195

defendants are afraid, lack the money and time, or accept whatever is handed them in the name of justice, despite misgivings they have or should have.

But what kind of lawyer is a good one to handle a drug case? He is not usually the lawyer who writes tax returns, transacts property purchases, or settles automobile accident cases. Lawyers, like other professionals, have become specialists.

A lawyer who has not followed the many state and federal criminal law decisions (such as those that relate to search and seizure, which are involved in most drug cases) will be lost in a drug offense trial. For example, in 1969 a young man was charged in a lower court of an eastern state with possession of marijuana and a number of other lesser offenses. By questioning a girlfriend who had smoked pot with the young man, the police had discovered where the boy hid grass in his apartment. On the basis of her information, the police applied for a search warrant. They told the clerk the girl's story, but kept her name a secret *even though she was willing to be* (in fact, her mother was willing for her to be) *the chief witness for the prosecution*. The clerk, who was not a lawyer as is often the case, wrote up an affidavit which more or less said: "An informer told the police that John Doe has marijuana in his house on Main Street." After the warrant was issued, the police made a raid and discovered a "green herblike substance," which was analyzed as marijuana. They arrested the young man and a friend who was visiting.

At the trial the defendant was represented by a lawyer who, although good at writing real estate contracts and deeds, was not a criminal lawyer. The prosecutor knew the warrant was illegal, as did the police. The judge knew the warrant was illegal because he had looked at the affidavit out of curiosity (he could not, however, rule on the warrant's validity until someone questioned it). Even the clerk knew the warrant was illegal, for he had been told so by the prosecutor. But the defendant's lawyer did not know. During the trial when the policeman who applied for the warrant began to testify, the lawyer representing the boy disappeared into the clerk's office and stayed there until the prosecutor finished his examination. The prosecutor expected the defense attorney to appear at any moment with a motion to suppress the evidence because the warrant was illegal. When the defense lawyer returned, the judge said, "This is the policeman who got the warrant. Do you want to cross-examine him?" The defense lawyer replied, "The warrant? The warrant, judge? I have no objections to the warrant." The judge, who is not allowed to lead a lawyer, did ask once again, "The policeman got the warrant. Do you have any questions about the warrant?" "No, judge," the lawyer responded quizzically, still unable to catch the hint. The case continued, and the defendant was found guilty.

The warrant in the above case would not have stood up as valid in 1791, when the Bill of Rights was passed, yet the defendant's lawyer was not aware of its invalidity. The judge is not allowed to tell a lawyer how to try his case. The prosecutor for various reasons did not inform the defense lawyer— his adversary in court—of the illegality of the warrant. He might have advised the defendant to get another lawyer and appeal, but no doubt the defendant would have been suspicious of his intent. The prosecutor knew that the police really had enough information to get a valid warrant, if they and the clerk had gone about their work correctly. He also knew that the court would probably give the boy probation with dismissal and clearance of the record after six months or a year. So the prosecutor rationalized and said nothing to the youth. But the point is that too many frantic parents, whose children are

197

charged with drug offenses, go to *a* lawyer rather than to a specialized lawyer who practices criminal law and has an interest in drug problems.

The majority of criminal cases become "dispositions"—that is, the defendant agrees to plead guilty if the prosecution will reduce the charges or recommend low sentences or probation, or both. Most criminal cases never go to trial, as dispositions are usually arrived at by the defense attorney and the prosecutor. With full knowledge of the "trial value" of their cases, they decide what to do on a plea of guilty. Often a probation officer confers with both sides, and until recently (maybe even now in some states) judges would join in the conference. It is almost invariably the defense attorney who approaches the prosecutor and says, "What can you do for us if my client pleads guilty?" Most prosecutors adopt the attitude that their duty is to present the evidence, good or bad, in the best way possible, whatever the outcome. Sometimes an agreement is reached before any court action, and at other times after a preliminary hearing to determine if evidence should be suppressed. Dispositions are considered "wins" for both sides. The prosecution gets a "guilty" or something near to it, and the defense gets a light sentence or probation. In drug cases the battle is often won or lost at the stage of the preliminary hearing (after the motion to suppress has been heard). If at the hearing everything is found to be in order—the search was legal and the accused was informed of his rights—so that drugs can be presented in court as evidence, there is not usually any great reason to go to trial. Instead, a disposition will be made.

The bargaining power in a disposition is dependent on a number of factors, chief of which is the so-called trial value of the case. If he is certain to be found guilty, the defendant is well advised to plead guilty. On the other hand, if the prosecution anticipates a serious fight, obviously he can reasonably expect a degree of leniency. All dispositions are subject to the judge's approval. Some judges never pay attention to recommendations; others always do, and some do only when they trust the attorneys who make them. It is essential, therefore, for the defense attorney to know how the judge feels about the prosecutor and his recommendations and what his decisions have been in similar cases. Sometimes judges are more sympathetic about certain offenses than about others, which means it is useful to know, if possible, how the judge feels about drugs—whether, for example, he thinks marijuana is as dangerous as heroin. A good trial lawyer will try to be aware of all the human frailties involved. Dispositions are not detrimental to the accused, *if* the defense attorney is good at his job. The defense attorney must be sensitive, intuitive, and well informed; for him the ability to dispose of cases is as necessary as the ability to try cases. Once the defendant has pleaded guilty or is found guilty by a judge or jury, his lawyer is presented the opportunity to be heard on disposition or sentencing —to tell the judge what he, the defense attorney, deems to be fair and suitable punishment. Here again a good criminal lawyer can make all the difference; he can make a reasonable plea and often enough secure for his client a good deal. On the other hand, a hostile lawyer can, through provocations and insults, drive a judge to a harsher penalty.

Dispositions are good compromises from the standpoint of *time*. The courts are overcrowded with cases, and judges like to get cases behind them. If every case called were to be tried, the present number of judges quadrupled would still have to sit day and night to hear all the cases. Prosecutors, whose positions are usually elective, often campaign on the number of cases handled and won and therefore are also anxious to dispose of cases. Trial, then, is a last resort.

A further problem in drug cases is selecting an unbiased jury, because most Americans are inclined to fear drugs, often enough for good reason. The defense attorney's judgment of what kind of jurors he wants for a particular case, if indeed he wants a jury at all, is very important. Today judges are often better informed than jurors about the dangers (or lack thereof) of marijuana. Like President Nixon, many judges believe that "... the answer is not more penalties. The answer is information." There are no hard and fast rules by which to select the most desirable jurors from the defendant's point of view. Unfortunately, the better informed people often try very hard to get out of jury duty or are vetoed by prosecutors. If judges have dealt severely with marijuana users—not pushers, but users—juries have an even more stringent record, often seeing the user as a potential "enemy of the people."

Because in each drug case the evidence, be it marijuana or heroin, must be analyzed, the question of the expertise of "expert witnesses" arises. The prosecutor has to prove that *in fact* the seized substance is, say, marijuana. The analysis is usually done by some state agency, perhaps a special branch of the police department or the food and drug section of a public health agency. Because there has been a tremendous increase in the number of analyses required and there are not enough competent chemists, some states allow a report of the analysis to be introduced by the prosecution. Other states require the chemist or other expert to testify. Joseph Oteri, the defense attorney in the *Leis and Weiss* case who has defended dozens and dozens of accused drug offenders, was asked what he would recommend to defense lawyers in drug cases. He replied that since 99 percent of drug cases involve a search and in at least a third of those the search can be shown illegal, lawyers should question the search in each case and also demand that the chemist be put on the stand for examination. A document should never go on the record unquestioned, if there is reason to doubt its accuracy. Chemists can be wrong or biased. If he is a member of the police department or works in conjunction with it, a chemist may indeed find results that please the police rather than the defendant. It is the prosecution's job to prove a man guilty beyond a reasonable doubt. But often, in fact, a lot of doubts raised by the defense, none of them conclusive in themselves, manage to create "reasonable doubt" and acquittal in the minds of a jury.

The judge ideally is very careful to assure that the defendant is not browbeaten into a plea. He will often examine a defendant who pleads guilty to determine that his plea is voluntary and made with the advice of counsel. Although he is not called upon to decide the facts in a jury case, the judge probably does so in his own mind. In the light of his own experience, he knows whether the case was a close one, whatever the verdict and does not need to hear that from the defense attorney at the time of disposition. A good criminal lawyer will take advantage of this last chance with the judge before sentencing—to emphasize any extenuating circumstances or other positive aspects of his client's case or record.

It is especially important that the defense attorney know just about all there is to know about his client—his school record, his service record, and any previous criminal record. In most serious cases the judge will have a probation sheet that provides at least those facts about the defendant. Defense lawyers usually have access to some parts of the probation report, which is prepared to aid the judge in sentencing. But often defense lawyers ask their clients if they have records, and

201

the clients reply "no," meaning "no, not in this city" or "not in this state." Yet, the judge's report includes records of the state and the FBI, which show any previous convictions.

In brief summary, what should a person accused of a drug offense do? Because the legal profession has become so specialized, it is almost impossible to map a course of action for the layman himself who is confronted with a legal problem regarding drugs. His best advice is to get a good criminal lawyer—the best criminal lawyer that he can afford. This advice, seemingly obvious, is too often overlooked. Drug offenses, in spite of some changes in recent laws, are still treated as criminal offenses. The accused person should also be aware of his right to call a lawyer the minute he is put in a "custodial situation"—that is, the minute that the police indicate that he is under arrest or that he is to be held indefinitely until they are satisfied in regard to his behavior.

If his case involves a raid, as most drug cases do, the defendant should be certain to get a good criminal lawyer as soon as possible. Beforehand, at the time of the police entry, he should ask to see their search warrant. If the people conducting a raid say they have a warrant, the occupant has a right to see it. If they do not have a warrant, the occupant has a right to refuse them entry until they produce one (unless they have substantial reasons—called "probable cause" in the law—to arrest and thus to make a search incidental to or in conjunction with that arrest). However, it is useless to argue about the validity of the warrant at the time of the search. No one, not even a lawyer, can prevent a warranted search in this respect. Warrants are challenged after the fact. Only after the search and the seizure of any evidence can the accused, through his lawyer, challenge the validity of the warrant. The pitfalls in this procedure are that the police through the search

202

have found drugs and think they can connect them to the accused. The defense is fighting the fact that the accused was, at least, close to these drugs, the possession of which is illegal. The only recourse the defense has in this "after the fact" hearing is to establish that the search was also illegal. This can be difficult when the accused appears to have been acting illegally by possessing the drugs.

The court system assumes, if not necessitates, lawyers to represent defendants. It rarely allows the accused to represent himself. "Tell it to the judge" is the name of the game, and the only people who can tell it to the judge are lawyers. Above all, the accused person should get the best criminal lawyer that he can afford.

All in all, "justice" can be a source of confusion and dismay. We demand from the courts the "law and order" we hear so much about and certainly have a right to seek. But how much can "the law" actually do? In December 1969 Judge Samuel Liebowitz of New York retired. He was well known as a tough judge, both in terms of his sentences and of the conduct in his court. Here is what he said on that occasion, a fitting end to a discussion of the legal aspects of drug use:

. . . the most interesting thing was my frustrations: the futility of a lot of it because prisons are an abject, absolute failure. Sixty-six per cent of the discharged prisoners come back and that ipso facto establishes the charge that prisons are a failure.

What can we do about it? Damn little.

The laws
themselves

This chapter lists the penalties for marijuana and other drug offenses in each of the states, including the District of Columbia. But first, some terms that require explanation are defined below. The law attaches meanings to certain words that may differ from their usual meanings.

Possession

Possession, which is any sort of control exercised over something, is usually proved by inference. For example, when marijuana is found in an apartment rented to John Smith, the inference is that John Smith is in *possession* of that marijuana. In most states he would have to prove otherwise.

Use

Some states have penalties for the *use* of marijuana or narcotic drugs. How *use* can be proved without also proving possession is not certain, but often the charge of *use* is utilized by by the courts to allow an accused to plead guilty to a lesser charge. In other words, although charged with both possession and *use,* the defendant for various reasons—a first offense or a search of questionable validity—may be allowed to plead guilty to *use* and avoid the usual felony conviction for possession.

Felony and misdemeanor

Each state has its own definition, based on the maximum sentence for an offense and where the sentence may be served, of what constitutes a *felony* and a *misdemeanor.* An offense that allows a maximum sentence to a county jail is usually a *misdemeanor* and an offense that brings a sentence in a state prison or a penitentiary is a *felony.*

Furnishing

Almost every method of transfer of illegal drugs from one person to another is covered by law and punished. *Furnishing* applies to the very common situation in which one person passes a joint to another person.

Minors

The definition of *minor* varies from state to state. In some states a *minor* is a person under twenty-one; in others, under nineteen; in some, under eighteen; and in some, under seventeen. The definition may differ according to legal purpose. For example, in Massachusetts a *minor* is a person under twenty-one, but in regard to the charge of contributing to the delinquency of a *minor,* a *minor* is under seventeen and in regard to the charge of statutory rape, a *minor* is under sixteen.

Suspension

Many states do not allow *suspension* of a sentence for various drug offenses. *Suspension* is an act whereby an accused, after being found guilty or pleading guilty, receives a sentence that need not now be served, but also is put on probation for a certain period of time, which is usually longer than the sentence. If he breaks the law at any time during the period of probation, even the last week or day, the convicted person must serve the sentence. For example, John Smith receives a two-year suspended sentence with five years probation for possession of marijuana. If after 4 years and 360 days he is again arrested for possession of marijuana or for some other offense, the *suspension* is lifted and John must serve the two-year sentence for the first offense in addition to whatever penalty he may receive for the second offense.

Probation

Probation, under which a convicted person has freedom pending good behavior, may be granted either with a suspended sentence or by itself—called *straight probation.* For example, John Smith is convicted of possession of one ounce of marijuana and given a two-year *straight probation.* He must comply with the terms of his *probation* as set out by the probation office or the court. These terms usually relate to keeping the probation office informed of his whereabouts and activities, but may include other conditions, such as being at home by a certain hour, seeing a psychiatrist, attending a drug clinic, or even attending school regularly.

Continuance with dismissal

Continuance with dismissal is an act whereby the trial of a case is postponed for a certain period of time—six months, a year, or whatever. If during that period the conduct of the accused is good, the case will be called forward and dismissed without trial. The advantage of this procedure, which is not possible in all states, is that the accused will not have the criminal record he would have for being found guilty or pleading guilty and receiving straight probation or a suspended sentence. A proposed federal law allows *continuance with dismissal* for first offenses of possession of marijuana, but terms it *conditional discharge.*

Parole

Parole is that procedure whereby a person is released under supervision from jail or prison before the expiration of his sentence. Rules for *parole* eligibility vary from state to state, but rarely is a sentence of five to ten years served for ten years. Most states have placed restrictions on *parole* eligibility for more serious drug offenses.

The laws on drugs, particularly marijuana, in the United States are listed by state below. Every drug offense in each state is not included, however, because of the principle emphasis on marijuana laws. The laws are up-to-date to 1969 for all states and to 1970 for most states.

The marijuana laws offer a glimpse into the nation's social and cultural values; in them is a microcosm of our attitudes toward right and wrong or acceptable and unacceptable behavior. The dry, weighty marijuana laws speak eloquently and sharply—about us and the system we somehow allow, perhaps desire, to exist.

Alabama

It is a felony to possess, sell, deliver, transport, or give away marijuana. A first offense is punishable by imprisonment for not less than five nor more than twenty years and a fine of up to $20,000.

A second offense, which includes an out-of-state conviction for any violation of any narcotic or marijuana law, is punishable by imprisonment for not less than ten nor more than forty years and a fine of up to $20,000.

If a person over eighteen sells, offers to sell, delivers, barters, or gives marijuana to a person under eighteen, he shall be punished by imprisonment for not less than ten nor more than forty years and a fine of up to $20,000.

There is no suspension or probation allowed for these sentences.

Alaska

To possess or to control marijuana or any depressant, stimulant, or hallucinogenic drug is a misdemeanor if the possession or control is for one's use; the penalty is imprisonment for not more than one year or a fine of up to $1,000, or both.

If the possession or control is for the purpose of sale "or other disposal to another person," it is a felony and punishable on a first offense by imprisonment for not more than twenty-five years or a fine of up to $20,000, or both; second and subsequent offenses are punishable by imprisonment for any term of years, or life, or a fine of up to $25,000, or both. The penalties for sale are the same.

The sale or "disposal of" marijuana or any depressant, stimulant, or hallucinogenic drug to a person under nineteen is a felony and punishable by imprisonment for any term of years, or life, or a fine of up to $25,000, or both.

There do not appear to be any restrictions on suspension, probation, or parole regarding these sentences.

The possession of LSD is similarly punished.

Arizona

The use of a narcotic, and that includes marijuana, is punishable on the first offense by one year in the county jail or probation for up to five years, but ninety days must be spent in

Arizona (continued)

jail. To grow, plant, cultivate, harvest, dry, process, or possess marijuana is punishable by imprisonment in the county jail for not more than one year or in state prison for not less than one year nor more than ten years or a fine of up to $1,000, or both.

A second offense is punishable by a sentence in state prison of not less than two nor more than twenty years.

A third or subsequent offense is punishable by five years to life, and five years has to be served.

The possession of marijuana for sale is punishable by not less than two nor more than ten years in state prison, and two years must be served.

A second offense of "possession for sale" (relating to marijuana or narcotics) is punishable by not less than five nor more than fifteen years in state prison and five years must be served.

A third or subsequent offense of possession for sale is punishable by ten years to life, and six years must be served.

Selling, furnishing, administering, transporting, importing, or offering or attempting to do the same is punishable by five years to life, and three years must be served.

A second offense is punishable by five years to life, and five years must be served.

A third offense is punishable by ten years to life, and ten years must be served.

Anyone over twenty-one who uses a minor to transport, carry, sell, prepare for sale, or peddle marijuana or anyone who sells, furnishes, administers, or gives marijuana to a minor, or offers or attempts to do the same is punished by ten years to life, and five years must be served.

A second offense is punishable by ten years to life, and ten years must be served.

A third or subsequent offense is punishable by fifteen years to life, and fifteen years must be served.

There is no probation or suspension for persons with previous offenses or for persons over twenty-one selling narcotics other than marijuana.

Second and subsequent offenses include any out-of-state (state or federal) convictions for similar offenses relating to marijuana or narcotics, if they are punishable as felonies in Arizona. For example, if possession of marijuana is a felony in Arizona and a person had previously been convicted in Alabama of possession and is now convicted in Arizona of selling marijuana, his previous conviction of possession can be used against him to make his offense in Arizona a second offense (even though the Alabama offense was only for possession and the second is for selling).

The quantity possessed must be usable, and ineffective seeds do not count.

Arkansas

It is a crime to possess, control, sell, purchase, prescribe, administer, dispense, or compound any narcotic drug, and that includes marijuana.

A first offense is punishable by a fine of up to $2,000 and imprisonment for not less than two nor more than five years.

A second offense is punishable by a fine of up to $2,000 and imprisonment for not less than five nor more than ten years.

A third or subsequent offense is punishable by a fine of up to $2,000 and imprisonment for not less than ten nor more than twenty years in the state penitentiary.

Second or subsequent offenses include out-of-state (state or federal) convictions that relate to narcotics or marijuana.

Except for first offenses there is no suspension of sentence or probation allowed, and parole cannot be granted until the minimum term is served.

211

California

The use of marijuana or being under the influence of marijuana is punishable by a county jail term of ninety days to one year. If probation is granted, then ninety days must be served.

Anyone who possesses marijuana is punished by imprisonment in the county jail for not more than one year or in state prison for not less than one nor more than ten years.

A second offense is punishable by not less than two nor more than twenty years in state prison, and two years must be served.

A third or subsequent offense is punishable by five years to life, and five years must be served.

Anyone who possesses marijuana for sale is punished by not less than two nor more than ten years in state prison, and two years must be served.

A second offense is punishable by not less than five nor more than fifteen years in prison, and three years must be served.

A third or subsequent offense is punishable by ten years to life in state prison, and six years must be served.

Transporting, importing, selling, furnishing, administering, or giving away of marijuana, or offering or attempting to do the same is punishable by five years to life in the state prison, and three years must be served.

A second offense carries the same penalty, but five years must be served.

A third or subsequent offense is punishable by ten years to life in the state prison, and ten years must be served.

A person over twenty-one who employs, hires, or uses a minor to carry, transport, sell, give away, prepare for sale, or peddle marijuana, or who sells, furnishes, gives, administers, or offers to do the same, or who induces a minor to use marijuana is punished by ten years to life in the state prison and is not eligible for release for at least five years.

A second offense carries the same penalty, but the eligibility for release is after ten years.

A third or subsequent offense is punishable by fifteen years to life, and fifteen years must be served.

The cultivation, harvesting, drying, or processing of marijuana is punishable by one to ten years in state prison, and one year must be served.

A second offense is punishable by two to twenty years, and two years must be served.

A third offense is punishable by five years to life, and five years must be served.

Note that a second offense includes any previous California conviction under this chapter which may be a felony (from possession up) and any out-of-state (state or federal) conviction which would be a felony had it occurred in California.

There is no probation or suspension on a second or subsequent offense. Persons over twenty-one convicted of selling or furnishing narcotic drugs other than marijuana to a minor cannot receive probation or a suspension of sentence.

Colorado

Use of, addiction to, or being under the influence of marijuana or narcotics, is punishable by not less than six months nor more than one year in the county jail. The possession, sale, purchase, control, receipt, manufacturing, prescribing, administering, compounding, or dispensing of marijuana and other narcotic drugs or conspiring to do the same is a felony punishable by not less than two nor more than fifteen years and a fine of up to $10,000.

A second offense is punishable by not less than five nor more than twenty years in prison and a fine of not more than $10,000.

A third or subsequent offense is punishable by imprisonment for not less than ten nor more than thirty years and a fine of up to $10,000.

Any one who intends to induce or aid another to use or possess marijuana or other narcotic drugs and who possesses it

213

Colorado (continued)

for sale, or sells it, or induces or attempts to induce another to use or administer it, or dispenses, or administers it, or employs, induces, or uses another to transport, carry, dispense, produce, or manufacture it, or induces or attempts to induce another to violate the narcotic drug law of Colorado, or conspires to do any of the above shall be punished by not less than ten nor more than twenty years for a first offense.

A second offense is punishable by not less than fifteen nor more than thirty years imprisonment.

A third offense is punishable by not less than twenty nor more than forty years imprisonment.

Minimum sentences must be served.

If the "other person" is under twenty-five, then the person intending to induce or aid him to use or possess narcotic drugs in any of the above ways shall be imprisoned for life for a first offense.

For a second offense he shall receive life imprisonment or death.

Subsequent offenses include out-of-state (state or federal) convictions for narcotics offenses, if they are felonies.

Federal conviction or acquittal for the same act is a bar to prosecution in Colorado. Marijuana seeds found must be capable of germination to convict for possession.

Connecticut

The possession or control of marijuana is punishable by a fine up to $1,000 or imprisonment for not more than one year, or both. Or the offender may be sentenced to the custody of the Commissioner of Correction for an indeterminate term not to exceed one year, and the Commissioner may release such person at any time.

214

The sale, prescribing, dispensing, manufacturing, compounding, transporting with intent to sell or dispense, possession with intent to sell or dispense, offering, giving, or administering to another of either a narcotic or a cannabis-type drug (including marijuana) is punishable by not less than five nor more than ten years in prison and a possible fine of up to $3,000 for a first offense, not less than ten nor more than fifteen years in prison and a possible fine of up to $5,000 for a second offense, and twenty-five years in prison for any subsequent offense.

Prosecutions may be suspended for "drug-dependent" people who seek and receive treatment. Whether the charges get dismissed after such treatment is a matter for each judge to decide.

If there is a federal prosecution for the same acts prohibited in Connecticut, there can be no prosecution.

Delaware

Possession of marijuana is punishable by not more than two years in prison and a fine of up to $500. If the accused is under twenty-one and bought the marijuana from a friend of at least one year who is believed to be under twenty-one and the accused is not a dealer in drugs, the penalty is not more than ninety days in confinement or a fine of up to $500, or both.

A subsequent offense is punishable by not more than five years in prison and a fine of up to $3,000.

The sale of marijuana is punishable by not less than five nor more than ten years in prison and a fine of from $1,000 to $10,000 for a first offense. If the accused is under twenty-one and bought the marijuana from a friend believed to be under twenty-one and the accused is not a dealer in drugs, the penalty is not more than two years in prison or up to $1,000, or both.

A second offense of selling is punishable by ten to twenty-five years in prison and a fine of from $5,000 to $50,000.

215

District of Columbia

Possession, manufacture, control, sale, prescribing, administering, dispensing, or compounding any narcotic drug (including marijuana) is punishable by imprisonment for not more than one year for the first offense or a fine of $100 to $1,000, or both.

A second or subsequent offense is punishable by not more than ten years in prison or a fine of $500 to $5,000, or both.

An accused cannot elect to be tried under these laws with their low penalty rather than under federal penalties. Note that the District of Columbia is peculiar in that all federal agencies, including the Bureau of Narcotics, are there and that Congress is its legislative body, so it is more than likely that federal charges would be brought in serious cases. If a person is tried under federal law, he cannot be tried by the District.

The amount of the narcotic in question must be a usable amount in order for a case to be brought.

Florida

The possession, manufacture, control, prescribing, administering, dispensing, or compounding of marijuana or any narcotic drug is a felony punishable by not more than five years in prison or a fine of up to $5,000, or both.

A second offense is punishable by not more than ten years and a fine of up to $10,000.

A third offense is punishable by not more than twenty years and a fine of up to $20,000.

Sale of marijuana or any narcotic drug is punishable by imprisonment for not more than ten years and a fine of up to $10,000.

A second offense is punishable by not less than ten nor more than twenty years and a fine of up to $20,000.

216

A third offense is punishable by not less than twenty years nor more than life and a fine of up to $20,000.

If the sale is to a person under twenty-one, the first offense is punishable by not less than ten years to life and a fine of up to $10,000.

A second offense is punishable by not less than ten years to life and a fine of up to $20,000.

A third or subsequent offense is punishable by not less than twenty years to life and a fine of up to $20,000.

If the seller is under twenty-one and has no previous record relating to narcotics, he is punished by not more than ten years and a fine of up to $10,000, or both.

Sentences for second or subsequent offenses of sale of marijuana and any offense of sale to a person under twenty-one by a person over twenty-one may not be suspended or deferred nor can probation be granted.

Georgia

The possession, control, sale, prescribing, administering manufacturing, dispensing, compounding, mixing, cultivating, growing, processing, or preparing of marijuana or any narcotic drug is punishable by a fine of up to $2,000 and imprisonment for not less than two nor more than five years on the first offense, and a fine of up to $3,000 and imprisonment for not less than five nor more than ten years for a second offense.

A third or subsequent offense is punishable by not less than ten nor more than twenty years in prison and a fine of up to $5,000.

Probation, suspension of sentence, and parole are not allowed for subsequent offenses until the minimum has been served.

The sale or giving away of a narcotic drug to a minor or

Georgia (continued)

the offer to do the same is punishable by life in the penitentiary unless the jury recommends not less than ten nor more than twenty years, and the judge may give less.

A second offense is punishable by death unless the jury recommends mercy, and then the penalty shall be life imprisonment. The jury may recommend not less than ten nor more than twenty years, but their recommendation in regard to years is not binding on the judge. Their recommendation of mercy is, however, binding.

No probation, suspension, or parole is allowed for these offenses.

Second and subsequent offenses include previous out-of-state convictions relating to narcotic drugs or marijuana.

Hawaii

The possession of marijuana is punishable by imprisonment for not more than one year or for not less than one year nor more than five years. (If the sentence is not more than one year, the offense is a misdemeanor; if the sentence is not less than one year nor more than five years, the offense is a felony.)

A second offense, which includes any felony offense within the Hawaii Uniform Narcotic Drug Act and any out-of-state offenses that would be a felony under the Act, is punishable by not less than two nor more than ten years in prison.

A third or subsequent offense, with the same conditions, is punishable by imprisonment for not less than five nor more than twenty years.

Second and subsequent offenders are not eligible for release on parole or otherwise until the minimum sentences are served.

Idaho

Possession of marijuana or any narcotic drug is punishable by not more than ten years in prison.

Possession for sale of marijuana or any narcotic drug is punishable by not more than fifteen years in prison.

The selling, transporting, importing, administering, or giving away of marijuana or any narcotic, or offering or attempting to do the same of marijuana or any narcotic is punishable by not more than ten years in prison.

Anyone who in any way solicits a minor to violate this act or in any way hires a minor to sell or give away marijuana or any narcotic or who sells or gives marijuana or any narcotic to a minor shall be punished by an imprisonment of not more than fifteen years.

Illinois

Use of, addiction to, or being under the influence of marijuana or other narcotic drugs is a misdemeanor punishable by ninety days to one year. Five years of probation may be granted, but ninety days confinement must be served.

Possession of 2.5 grams or less is punishable by imprisonment (but not in a penitentiary) for not more than one year or a fine of up to $1,500, or both.

Possession, control, manufacture, or compounding of more than 2.5 grams of marijuana or any narcotic drug is punishable by imprisonment for not less than two nor more than ten years and a fine of up to $5,000.

The sale, prescribing, administering, trafficking, or dispensing of marijuana or any narcotic drug is punishable by ten years to life imprisonment.

219

Illinois (continued)

A second or subsequent offense is punishable by life imprisonment. No probation or suspension is allowed for this offense.

Anyone who solicits, endorses, encourages, or intimidates anyone under twenty-one to violate the Narcotic Drug Act can receive from two to five years in the penitentiary.

Second offenses include out-of-state offenses that are felonies and any other narcotics offense in Illinois.

There is a special provision for a person who offers to provide narcotics to another person and provides instead non-narcotics; this offense is punishable by one to ten years.

Indiana

Possession or control of marijuana or any narcotic is punishable by not less than two nor more than ten years in prison and a fine of up to $1,000.

A second offense is punishable by not less than five nor more than twenty years in prison and a fine of up to $2,000.

Possession or control of marijuana or any narcotic drug with intent to sell, barter, exchange, give, dispense, or aid in the same is punishable by not less than five nor more than twenty years in prison and a fine of up to $2,000. A second offense is punishable by not less than twenty years nor more than life in prison and a fine of up to $5,000.

The sale, manufacture, prescribing, administering, dispensing, or compounding of marijuana or any narcotic drug is punishable by not less than five nor more than twenty years.

A second or subsequent offense is punishable by twenty years to life in prison and a fine of up to $5,000.

Second offenses include previous out-of-state convictions for

220

the sale, manufacture, prescribing, administering, dispensing, or compounding of any narcotic drug (including marijuana) or soliciting another person to solicit a third person to do the same.

No suspension of sentence is allowed when the sale is to someone under twenty-one, or when the conviction is for the sale, manufacture, dispensing, prescribing, administering, or compounding of marijuana or any narcotic drug, or when the conviction is for possession or control with intent to sell, give, dispense, barter, or exchange marijuana or any narcotic drug.

Iowa

Possession of or purchase of marijuana or attempt to purchase marijuana for personal use is punishable by up to six months in jail or a fine of up to $1,000.

Possession of or purchase of marijuana or attempt to purchase marijuana for sale is punishable by not less than two nor more than five years in prison and a fine of up to $2,000.

A second offense of either kind of possession is punishable by not less than five nor more than ten years and a fine of up to $2,000.

A third offense of either kind of possession is punishable by not less than ten nor more than twenty years and a fine of up to $2,000.

Possession of other narcotic drugs and selling of any narcotic drug (including marijuana) is punishable by not less than two nor more than five years and a fine of up to $2,000.

A second offense is punishable by not less than five nor more than ten years and a fine of up to $2,000.

A third offense is punishable by not less than ten nor more than twenty years.

Sale to a minor is punishable by not less than five nor more than twenty years.

Kansas

The possession, sale, control, manufacture, prescribing, administering, dispensing, or compounding of marijuana or any narcotic drug is a felony punishable by imprisonment and hard labor for not more than seven years.

If convicted or acquitted in a federal court for any of the above resulting from the same incident, a person may not be prosecuted.

Kentucky

The use of marijuana or any narcotic drug or being under its influence is punishable by confinement in jail for twelve months. Probation is allowed if the accused enters an institution for treatment.

Possession of marijuana or any narcotic drug is a felony punishable by not less than two nor more than ten years in the penitentiary and a fine of up to $20,000.

Second or subsequent offenses are punishable by not less than five nor more than twenty years and fines of up to $20,000.

The sale, manufacture, prescribing, administering, dispensing, or compounding of marijuana or any narcotic drug is punishable by not less than five nor more than twenty years and a fine of up to $20,000 for a first offense, not less than ten nor more than forty years and a fine of up to $20,000 for a second offense.

The sale, supply, prescribing, administering, dispensing, or furnishing of marijuana or any narcotic or causing the same to be done to a person under twenty-one is punishable by twenty years to life imprisonment and a fine of up to $20,000. This sentence may not be suspended, postponed, or made subject to probation.

Suspension, probation, or postponement is not possible when a person has been previously convicted on an out-of-state narcotics offense.

Louisiana

Possession, control, or manufacture of marijuana or any narcotic drug by a person under twenty-one is punishable by not more than ten years in prison with or without hard labor. Suspension, probation, and parole of sentence are allowed.

Possession, control, or manufacture of marijuana or any narcotic drug by a person over twenty-one is punishable by not less than five nor more than fifteen years imprisonment at hard labor. Suspension, probation, and parole are allowed only for first offenders.

Selling, giving, administering, or delivering marijuana or any narcotic drug by a person under twenty-one is punishable by imprisonment at hard labor for not less than five nor more than fifteen years. There is no suspension, probation, or parole.

Selling, giving, administering, or delivering marijuana or any narcotic by a person over twenty-one is punishable by imprisonment at hard labor for not less than ten nor more than fifty years. There is no suspension, probation, or parole.

Selling, giving, or administering marijuana or any narcotic drug to a person under twenty-one is punishable by death or imprisonment at hard labor for not less than thirty nor more than ninety-nine years (the choice is up to the jury). There is no suspension, probation, or parole.

Maine

The possession, control, manufacture, growing, or cultivating of marijuana or peyote is punishable by imprisonment for not

223

Maine (continued)

more than eleven months and a fine of up to $1,000 for the first offense, and not more than two years in prison and a fine of up to $2,000 for a subsequent offense.

Knowingly being in the presence of marijuana or peyote has the same punishment as a first offense for possession.

The sale, furnishing, delivering, or giving of marijuana or peyote to a person over twenty-one is punishable by imprisonment for not less than one nor more than five years. If the recipient is eighteen to twenty, the penalty is not less than two nor more than six years. If the recipient is under eighteen, the penalty is not less than three nor more than eight years.

A subsequent offense is punishable by not less than four nor more than ten years.

If the person selling, furnishing, delivering, or giving is under twenty-one, the penalty is not less than one nor more than five years. The age of the recipient does not matter in this case.

Maryland

It is a felony to possess, control, sell, prescribe, administer, dispense, or compound any narcotic drug (including marijuana), and no one can grow, mix, compound, cultivate, produce, or prepare a narcotic drug without a license.

A first offense is punishable by not less than two nor more than five years in prison and a fine of up to $1,000.

A second offense is punishable by not less than five nor more than ten years in prison and a fine of up to $2,000.

A third or subsequent offense is punishable by not less than ten nor more than twenty years in prison and a fine of up to $3,000.

Sentences may not be suspended nor parole or probation given until the minimum is served for second and subsequent offenses. Second and subsequent offenses include out-of-state (federal and state) convictions relating to narcotic drugs or marijuana.

Addiction is not a crime in Maryland.

Massachusetts

Knowingly being present where marijuana or any narcotic drug is kept or knowingly being in the company of a person in possession of marijuana or any narcotic drug is a felony punishable by not more than five years in the state prison or the house of correction for up to two years or a fine of not less than $500 nor more than $5,000.

The possession of marijuana or any narcotic drug is punishable by a fine of up to $1,000 or not more than three and one-half years in prison or two and one-half years in the house of correction.

Possession of marijuana or any narcotic drug except heroin with intent to sell is punishable by not less than five nor more than ten years in prison.

A second or subsequent offense is punishable by not less than ten nor more than twenty-five years in prison. The sentence cannot be suspended nor parole or probation given for the second or subsequent offense.

The sale of any narcotic drug (including marijuana) except heroin is punishable by not less than five nor more than ten years in prison.

A second or subsequent offense is punishable by not less than ten nor more than twenty-five years. There is no suspension of this sentence for a second or subsequent offense, and probation or parole cannot be granted until the minimum sentence is served.

225

Massachusetts (continued)

Inducing or attempting to induce another to use a narcotic drug (including marijuana) is punishable by not less than ten nor more than twenty-five years in prison.

A second or subsequent offense is punishable by not less than twenty nor more than fifty years in prison. There is no suspension of sentence, probation, or parole until the minimum is served.

Sale to a minor or using a minor to carry, dispense, or produce a narcotic drug (including marijuana) or dispensing or administering a narcotic drug (including marijuana) to a minor is punishable by not less than ten nor more than twenty years in prison.

A second offense is punishable by not less than twenty nor more than fifty years. Suspension of sentence is not allowed, and parole or probation cannot be granted until the minimum is served.

The penalties for heroin offenses are higher.

Michigan

Possession, control, prescribing, administering, dispensing, or compounding of any narcotic drug (including marijuana) is a felony punishable by not more than ten years in prison or a fine of up to $5,000.

Sale of marijuana or any narcotic drug is punishable by not less than twenty years nor more than life.

Minnesota

The possession, control, sale, prescribing, manufacture, administering, dispensing, or compounding of marijuana or any narcotic

226

drug is punishable by imprisonment for not less than five nor more than twenty years in prison and a fine of up to $10,000.

The sale, prescribing, dispensing, administering, or furnishing of marijuana or any narcotic drug to a minor under the age of eighteen is punishable by not less than ten nor more than forty years in prison and a fine of up to $20,000.

The provisions for second and subsequent offenders were repealed.

Mississippi

The possession, control, manufacture, prescribing, administering, compounding, or dispensing of marijuana or any narcotic drug is punishable by a fine of up to $2,000 and imprisonment for not less than two nor more than five years.

A second offense is punishable by a fine of up to $2,000 and imprisonment for not less than five nor more than ten years.

A third or subsequent offense is punishable by a fine of $2,000 and imprisonment for not less than ten nor more than twenty years.

The sale, exchange, barter, supplying, or giving of marijuana or narcotic drugs is punishable by a fine of not more than $2,000 and imprisonment for not less than five nor more than ten years.

A second offense is punishable by a fine of $2,000 and imprisonment for not less than ten nor more than twenty years.

A third offense is punishable by life imprisonment.

Sale or supply to a minor is punishable by a fine of not more than $20,000 and imprisonment for not less than twenty years to life.

Except for the first offense of possession, control, etc., there is no probation or parole or suspension of sentence until the minimum term is served.

Second and subsequent offenses include out-of-state convictions relating to marijuana or narcotic drugs.

227

Missouri

The possession, control, prescribing, administering, manufacture, dispensing, or compounding of marijuana or any narcotic drug or the possession of any apparatus or device for the use of narcotic drugs is punishable by a jail sentence of not less than six months nor more than one year or a prison sentence of not more than twenty years on a first offense.

A second offense is punishable by not less than five years nor more than life in prison.

A third or subsequent offense is punishable by imprisonment for not less than ten years nor more than life.

Selling, giving, or delivering of marijuana or any narcotic drug is punishable by not less than five years nor more than life in prison for a first offense.

A second offense is punishable by not less than ten years nor more than life.

If the sale, giving, or delivering is to a minor (under twenty-one), the death penalty may be imposed. Parole, probation, or suspension of sentence or any form of judicial clemency can be granted only for first offenders for possession, and then only if the accused has never been convicted of any felony. Second offenses include out-of-state convictions and in-state felony convictions relating to marijuana or narcotics.

Montana

Possession of dangerous drugs (including marijuana and other hallucinogenic, depressant, stimulant, or narcotic drugs) is punishable by not more than five years in prison. If the accused is twenty-one or under, the sentence for a first violation is "presumed to be entitled to a deferred imposition of sentence."

Anyone convicted of possession can be alternatively sentenced to a treatment center for not less than six months nor more than two years, if he is an excessive or habitual user of dangerous drugs.

Sale of dangerous drugs, which includes manufacture, preparation, cultivation, compounding, or processing, is punishable by imprisonment for not less than one year nor more than life. Again, a person twenty-one or under is "presumed to be entitled to a deferred imposition of sentence."

Nebraska

The possession of less than eight ounces of marijuana or less than twenty-five marijuana cigarettes is punishable by a mandatory jail sentence of seven days with instruction on drug abuse. A subsequent offense is punishable by not less than one nor more than five years in prison.

Possession of eight ounces or more of marijuana or of twenty-five or more marijuana cigarettes or possession with intent to sell is punishable by imprisonment for not less than one nor more than five years.

Sale of marijuana is punishable by not less than two nor more than five years.

Nevada

The possession, control, manufacture, prescribing, administering, dispensing, or compounding of any narcotic drug (including marijuana) is punishable for a first offense by not less than one nor more than six years in prison and a possible fine of up to $2,000.

A second offense is punishable by not less than one nor more than ten years in prison and a possible fine of up to $2,000.

229

Nevada (continued)

A third or subsequent offense is punishable by not less than one nor more than twenty years and a possible fine of up to $5,000.

The sale, exchange, barter, supply, or giving away of marijuana or any narcotic drug is punishable by not less than one nor more than twenty years and a possible fine of up to $5,000 for a first offense. Probation is allowed if the offender is under twenty-one.

A second offense is punishable by life imprisonment, without possibility of parole or probation, and a fine of up to $5,000.

The sale, exchange, barter, supply, or giving away of marijuana or a narcotic drug to a person under twenty-one is punishable by life in prison with eligibility for parole after seven years and a possible fine of up to $5,000. Probation is not allowed.

A second or subsequent offense is punishable by life in prison without possibility of parole or probation.

The supply of marijuana or narcotic drugs to another person with knowledge that he intends to sell, exchange, barter, supply, or give them away is punishable by life in prison with eligibility for parole after seven years and a possible fine of $5,000. For a second offense there is no possibility of parole.

New Hampshire

Possession or control of marijuana, amphetamines, barbiturates, cocaine, morphine, and hallucinogenic drugs—called "controlled" drugs in New Hampshire—is punishable by imprisonment for not more than one year or a fine of up to $500, or both.

230

A second or subsequent offense is punishable by not more than three years in prison or a fine of up to $1,000, or both.

Being in the presence of a controlled drug or of a person who is in possession of a controlled drug is punishable by not more than six months in prison or a fine of up to $500, or both.

A second or subsequent offense is punishable by imprisonment for not more than one year or a fine of up to $500, or both.

The manufacture, sale, dispensing, compounding, or transporting with intent to sell or offering, giving, or administering to another of a controlled drug is punishable by imprisonment for not more than ten years or a fine of up to $2,000, or both.

A subsequent offense is punishable by not more than fifteen years in prison or a fine of up to $5,000, or both.

New Jersey

Possession, control, sale, purchase, administering, prescribing, dispensing, or compounding marijuana or any narcotic drug is punishable by not less than two nor more than fifteen years in prison and a fine of up to $2,000 for a first offense, not less than five nor more than twenty-five years and a fine of up to $5,000 for a second offense, and not less than ten nor more than life and a fine of up to $5,000 for a third or subsequent offense.

If a person over twenty-one sells, gives, administers, or dispenses marijuana or any narcotic drug to a person under eighteen, the penalty is not less than two years nor more than life in prison and a fine of from $2,000 to $10,000.

Out-of-state convictions relating to narcotics count as second and subsequent offenses. [Although marijuana was deleted in reference to out-of-state convictions, marijuana offenses still may be included for second or subsequent offenses because New Jersey considers marijuana a narcotic.]

231

New Mexico

The use of marijuana is a misdemeanor punishable by jail for less than one year or a fine of up to $1,000, or both.

Possession of one ounce or less of *cannabis sativa L* (including marijuana, but not hashish or THC) is punishable by less than one year in jail or a fine of up to $1,000, or both.

A second offense is a fourth-degree felony punishable by not less than one nor more than five years or a fine of up to $5,000, or both.

A third or subsequent offense is a third-degree felony punishable by not less than two nor more than ten years and a fine of up to $5,000, or both.

Possession or control of more than one ounce of *cannabis sativa L* (or any amount of hashish, THC, or other narcotic drug) is punishable by not less than two nor more than ten years in prison and a fine of up to $2,000.

A second offense is punishable by not less than five nor more than twenty years in prison and a fine of up to $2,000.

A subsequent offense is punishable by not less than ten nor more than forty years in prison and a fine of up to $2,000.

Sale or otherwise disposing to another is punishable as follows: for the first offense, imprisonment for not less than ten nor more than twenty years and a fine of up to $5,000; for a second offense, imprisonment for not less than twenty nor more than forty years and a fine of up to $10,000; and for subsequent offenses, imprisonment for life and a fine of up to $20,000.

If the other is a minor and the seller or "disposer" is over twenty-one, the penalty is not less than twenty years nor more than life and a fine of up to $10,000.

If anyone over eighteen sells to a person under eighteen, he shall be punished by not less than ten years and up to life imprisonment or death, if the jury so decides.

Possession of less than one ounce and use are the only sentences that may be suspended, paroled, or given probation. Otherwise, the minimum must be served.

New York

Possession of a dangerous drug (including marijuana) is punishable by a definite sentence not to exceed one year and a fine of up to $1,000.

Possession with intent to sell a dangerous drug (including marijuana) is punishable by a fixed term of not more than four years and a possible fine.

Possession with intent to sell a narcotic drug, twenty-five or more cannabis cigarettes, one-eighth ounce or more of heroin, morphine, or cocaine, one-fourth ounce or more of cannabis, one-half ounce or more of opium, one-half ounce or more of other narcotic drugs or mere possession of the same is punishable by a fixed term of not more than seven nor less than three years in prison and a possible fine. A definite term of one year or less can be given in special circumstances.

Possession of one hundred or more cannabis cigarettes, one or more ounces of heroin, morphine, cocaine, or cannabis, or two or more ounces of opium or of any other narcotic drug is punishable by not less than five nor more than fifteen years in prison and a possible fine.

Possession of eight or more ounces of heroin, cocaine, morphine, or opium is punishable by not more than twenty-five years nor less than one-third of twenty-five years in prison and a possible fine.

Possession of sixteen ounces or more of heroin, cocaine, morphine, or opium is punishable by a minimum sentence of not less than fifteen nor more than twenty-five years and a maximum of life imprisonment and a possible fine.

Sale of a dangerous drug (including marijuana) is punishable by not more than seven nor less than three years in prison.

233

New York (continued)

A definite term of one year or less can be given in special circumstances.

Sale of a narcotic drug is punishable by not less than five nor more than fifteen years in prison and a possible fine.

Sale of a narcotic drug or of eight ounces or more of heroin, morphine, cocaine, or opium to a person under twenty-one is punishable by not more than twenty-five years nor less than one-third of twenty-five years and a possible fine.

Sale of a narcotic drug consisting of ten or more ounces of heroin, cocaine, morphine, or opium is punishable by a minimum of not less than fifteen nor more than twenty-five years and a maximum of life imprisonment.

In all cases fines are possible if the accused has made money through the commission of the crime, and the fines can be up to double the amount gained in the transaction.

North Carolina

Possession of one gram or less of marijuana is a misdemeanor punishable by fine or imprisonment for a term not exceeding two years, or both.

Possession of more than one gram of marijuana or other narcotic drug (including LSD) is punishable by up to five years in prison or a fine of up to $1,000, or both, for a first offense.

A second offense is punishable by not less than five nor more than ten years in prison and a fine of up to $2,000.

A third or subsequent offense is punishable by fifteen years to life in prison and a fine of up to $3,000.

The punishment for growing opium or marijuana is the same as the above.

Second offenses include any out-of-state convictions relating to the sale, use, or possession of narcotic drugs or marijuana.

North Dakota

The possession, growing, selling, trading, furnishing, or giving away of marijuana is punishable by not less than six months in the county jail nor more than two years in prison or a fine of up to $2,000, or both.

A second or subsequent offense is punishable by up to five years in prison or a fine of up to $2,000, or both.

The sale, furnishing, trading, or giving away of marijuana by a person over eighteen to a person under eighteen or the use of a person under eighteen to sell, etc., is punishable by imprisonment for not less than five nor more than ten years.

The possession, control, sale, prescribing, administering, compounding, dispensing, furnishing, trading, or giving away of a narcotic drug (other than marijuana) is punishable by imprisonment at hard labor for not more than ninety-nine years.

Ohio

The production, manufacture, growing, processing or cultivation of marijuana, cannabis, opium, or coca leaves is punishable by imprisonment for not less than two nor more than five years and a fine of up to $10,000 for a first offense.

A second offense is punishable by not less than five nor more than ten years in prison and a fine of up to $10,000.

A third or subsequent offense is punishable by not less than ten nor more than twenty years in prison and a fine of up to $10,000.

Possession or control of marijuana or any narcotic drug is

235

Ohio (continued)

punishable by not less than two nor more than fifteen years in prison and a fine of up to $10,000 for a first offense.

A second offense is punishable by not less than five nor more than twenty years in prison and a fine of up to $10,000.

A third or subsequent offense is punishable by not less than ten nor more than thirty years in prison and a fine of up to $10,000.

Possession for sale of marijuana or any narcotic drug is punishable by imprisonment for not less than ten nor more than twenty years for a first offense, not less than fifteen nor more than thirty years for a second offense, and not less than twenty nor more than forty years for a third or subsequent offense.

The sale of marijuana or any narcotic drug is punishable by not less than twenty nor more than forty years in prison.

Dispensing or administering marijuana or any narcotic drug to a minor is punishable by not less than thirty years nor more than life in prison.

Whoever knowingly has carnal knowledge of a person under the influence of a narcotic drug (including marijuana) is punished the same as one who has possession of marijuana or a narcotic drug.

Oklahoma

Knowingly permitting the growth of marijuana is a felony punishable by a fine of up to $1,000 and one year in the penitentiary. If marijuana is grown on your land, it is your duty to destroy it; and if you do not, the County Commissioner will, and he will charge you for its destruction.

To sell, possess, use, plant, cultivate, protect, harvest, prepare, cure, or give away marijuana in any form or to offer to sell, furnish, or give away marijuana in any form is punishable by not more than seven years in prison.

If the offense is selling, giving, furnishing, delivering, or exchanging to a person under twenty-one, the penalty is not more than twenty years for a first offense and not less than five years nor more than life for a second or subsequent offense.

By a 1969 act of the legislature, a student possessing any prohibited drug may be barred from any state campus.

Oregon

The use of narcotic or dangerous drugs (including marijuana) or being under their influence is punishable by not more than one year in the county jail or probation for up to five years. The specific drug used does not have to be proved.

The possession, control, sale, prescribing, administering, dispensing, or compounding of marijuana is punishable by imprisonment for one year in the county jail or for up to ten years in the penitentiary or a fine of up to $5,000 or both.

Pennsylvania

The using, taking, or administering of any narcotic drug (including marijuana) is a misdemeanor punishable by not more than one year in prison or a fine of up to $5,000.

A second offense is punishable by not more than three years in prison and a fine of up to $25,000.

The possession of marijuana or any narcotic is punishable by imprisonment for not less than two nor more than five years and a fine of up to $2,000, not less than five nor more than ten years and a fine of up to $5,000 for a second offense, and not

237

Pennsylvania (continued)

less than ten nor more than thirty years and a fine of up to $7,500 for a third offense.

To sell, dispense, or give away marijuana or any narcotic drug is punishable by imprisonment for not less than five nor more than twenty years and a fine of up to $5,000, not less than ten nor more than thirty years and a fine of up to $15,000 for a second offense, and a term of life and a fine of up to $30,000 for a third offense.

Second offenses include out-of-state convictions relating to the possession or sale of narcotics.

Rhode Island

Possession of marijuana or any narcotic drug is punishable by imprisonment for not more than fifteen years and a fine of up to $10,000 for a first offense, not more than twenty years and a fine of up to $10,000 for a second offense, and not more than thirty years and a fine of up to $10,000 for a third or subsequent offense.

Possession with intent to sell marijuana or any narcotic is punishable by imprisonment for not more than twenty years for a first offense, not more than thirty years for a second offense, and not more than forty years for a third or subsequent offense.

To sell, furnish, give away, or deliver marijuana or any narcotic drug is punishable by imprisonment for not more than forty years.

To sell, furnish, give away, or deliver marijuana or any narcotic drug to a person under twenty-one is punishable by not more than life imprisonment. There is no probation allowed for this latter offense.

238

South Carolina

The possession, control, sale, prescribing, manufacturing, administering, dispensing, or compounding of marijuana or any narcotic drug is punishable by not more than two years in prison or a fine of up to $2,000, or both, for a first offense, not less than two nor more than five years or a fine of from $2,000 to $5,000, or both, for a second offense, and not less than ten nor more than twenty years for a third or subsequent offense, without benefit of suspension of sentence, probation, or parole until ten years have been served.

To sell, furnish, or give marijuana or other narcotic drugs to a person under eighteen is punishable by five years imprisonment at hard labor or a fine of up to $5,000, or both, for a first offense, and ten years at hard labor (which is mandatory without suspension, probation, or parole) for a second or subsequent offense. If the offender is himself under eighteen, the sentence is discretionary with the court.

There is no prosecution if there was acquittal or conviction in the federal court for the same offense.

South Dakota

A first offense for possession of one ounce or less of marijuana is punishable by imprisonment for not more than one year or a fine of up to $500, or both.

The possession, control, manufacture, dispensing, compounding, administering, or purchase of more than one ounce of marijuana or any amount of any other narcotic drug is punishable by not less than two nor more than five years and a fine of up to $5,000 for a first offense, not less than five nor more than ten years and a fine of up to $10,000 for a second offense, and not

239

South Dakota (continued)

less than ten nor more than twenty years and a fine of up to $20,000 for a third or subsequent offense. Only a first offender is eligible for a suspended sentence, probation, or parole. Other offenders are eligible for parole at the end of the minimum term.

The sale, exchange, bartering, supplying, or giving away of marijuana or narcotic drugs is punishable by imprisonment for not less than five nor more than ten years for a first offense, and not less than ten nor more than twenty years for a second or subsequent offense. No parole, probation, or suspension of sentence is allowed until the minimum sentence has been served.

Second and subsequent offenses include out-of-state convictions relating to narcotic drugs or marijuana.

If acquitted or convicted for the same offense under federal law, a person cannot be prosecuted.

Tennessee

The possession, control, manufacture, sale, prescribing, administering, dispensing, or compounding of any narcotic drug or marijuana is a felony punishable by not less than two nor more than five years and a fine of up to $500 for a first offense, not less than five nor more than ten years and a fine of up to $500 for a second offense, and not less than ten nor more than twenty years and a fine of up to $500 for a third offense.

Second and subsequent offenses include out-of-state convictions relating to marijuana or narcotic drugs.

If convicted or acquitted in a federal court for the same offense, a person cannot be prosecuted.

240

Texas

The possession, control, prescribing, dispensing, or compounding of marijuana or any narcotic drug is punishable by imprisonment for not less than two years nor more than life for a first offense, and not less than ten years nor more than life for a second or subsequent offense. No suspended sentence, probation, or parole is allowed.

To sell, barter, trade, administer, give, or furnish marijuana or any narcotic drug, or offer to do the same is punishable by not less than five years nor more than life for a first offense, and not less than ten years nor more than life for a second or subsequent offense. No probation, parole, or suspended sentence is allowed for second offenses.

If a person over twenty-one sells, furnishes, administers, trades, barters, or gives marijuana or any narcotic drug to a person under twenty-one, or offers to do the same, or hires a person under twenty-one to sell, carry, prepare for sale, or peddle marijuana or any narcotic drug, he is punished by not less than five years nor more than life in prison for a first offense, and not less than ten years nor more than life or the death penalty for a second or subsequent offense. No parole, probation, or suspension of sentence is allowed for second offenses.

Utah

To use or be under the influence of marijuana or any narcotic drug is a misdemeanor punishable by not less than six months nor more than one year in jail or probation for up to five years if six months in jail is served.

The possession (which includes just about everything from

241

Utah (continued)

holding the drug in your hand to being around it), planting, cultivating, harvesting, drying, or processing of marijuana is punishable by not less than six months in jail. Probation is allowed for first and second offenses.

A third offense is punishable by not less than six months in jail or not less than one nor more than five years in prison.

Possession for sale of marijuana is punishable by imprisonment for not less than two nor more than ten years, with no parole eligibility until two years have been served, for a first offense, and not less than five nor more than fifteen years, with no parole eligibility until three years have been served, for a second offense.

A third or subsequent offense is punishable by imprisonment for from ten years to life, with no parole eligibility until six years have been served.

Selling, furnishing, giving away, transporting, or importing marijuana or attempting to do so is punishable by imprisonment for five years to life, with no parole eligibility until three years have been served.

The same punishment applies to second offenses except that parole eligibility begins after five years have been served.

A third or subsequent offense is punishable by ten years to life in prison, with no parole eligibility until ten years have been served.

Selling, furnishing, giving away, or administering marijuana to a minor, or offering to do the same, or inducing a minor to use marijuana, or using a minor to sell, prepare, or peddle marijuana is punishable by ten years to life in prison with no eligibility for parole until after five years have been served.

The same punishment applies to second offenses, except that parole eligibility begins after ten years have been served.

A third offense is punishable by fifteen years to life with no parole eligibility until fifteen years have been served.

Second offenses include in-state convictions relating to marijuana or narcotics and out-of-state convictions relating to marijuana or narcotics, except those which would be misdemeanors in Utah (i.e., a first offense of use or being under the influence).

Vermont

Persons in possession of marijuana or a depressant or stimulant drug may be sentenced to any state institution, except the state prison, for not more than six months or fined up to $500, or both.

Persons in possession of narcotic drugs or hallucinogenic drugs may be sentenced to any state institution, except state prison, for not more than one year or fined $500, or both.

A second or subsequent offense for possession of marijuana, depressants, stimulants, narcotics, or hallucinogenics *shall* be sentenced to any state institution, including state prison, for not more than two years or fined up to $2,000, or both.

Possession with intent to sell or possession of twenty-five or more marijuana cigarettes, one-eighth ounce of heroin, morphine, or cocaine, one-half ounce or more of marijuana, one-half ounce or more of opium, one hundred times the manufacturer's recommended maximum dose of a depressant or stimulant, five hundred micrograms of LSD, fifty milligrams or more of psilocybin, seven hundred milligrams or more of mescaline, six milligrams of methyl-phenylethylamine, or two hundred milligrams of dimethyltryptamine (DMT) is punishable by not more than two years in state prison or a fine of up to $2,000, or both.

Possession of one hundred marijuana cigarettes, one ounce or more of heroin, cocaine, or morphine, two ounces or more of marijuana, three hundred times the recommended dose of stim-

243

Vermont (continued)

ulants or depressants, one thousand micrograms of LSD, one hundred milligrams or more of psilocybin, seven hundred milligrams or more of mescaline, twelve milligrams or more of methyl-phenylethylamine, or four hundred milligrams of di-methyltryptamine (DMT) is punishable by imprisonment in state prison for not more than five years and a fine of up to $5,000.

The sale of any regulated drugs (including all drugs mentioned above) to a minor under eighteen is punishable by imprisonment for not more than five years and a fine of up to $10,000.

A second offense is punishable by not less than ten nor more than twenty-five years and a fine of up to $25,000.

Virginia

The possession, control, sale, manufacture, prescribing, administering, dispensing, or compounding of marijuana or any narcotic drug is punishable by imprisonment for not less than three nor more than five years and a fine of up to $1,000 for a first offense, not less than five nor more than ten years and a fine of up to $2,000 for a second offense, and not less than ten nor more than thirty years and a fine of up to $3,000 for a third or subsequent offense.

Possession of twenty-five grains or more of marijuana or any narcotic drug is punishable by not less than twenty and not more than forty years and a fine of not more than $5,000.

The sale, barter, peddling, exchange, dispensing, or supplying of marijuana or any narcotic drug to a minor is punishable by not less than ten nor more than thirty years and a fine of up to $1,000. No suspension of sentence is allowed.

Second offenses include out-of-state convictions relating to sale, use, or possession of marijuana or narcotic drugs.

Washington

Possession of marijuana is punishable by a jail term for not more than six months or a fine of up to $500, or both, for a first offense, not more than one year or a fine of $1,000, or both, for a second offense, and not more than ten years and a fine of up to $10,000 for a third or subsequent offense.

Possession with intent to sell and the sale of marijuana are punishable by not less than three nor more than ten years in prison and a fine of up to $5,000. Possession of more than forty grams creates a presumption that there is intent to sell.

A sale or other transaction with a minor is punishable by not more than twenty years in prison and a fine of up to $50,000.

West Virginia

The possession, control, sale, prescribing, administering, dispensing, or compounding of marijuana or any narcotic drug is punishable by imprisonment for not less than two nor more than five years and a fine of up to $1,000, not less than five nor more than ten years and a fine of up to $5,000 for a second offense, and not less than ten nor more than twenty years and a fine of up to $10,000 for a third offense.

The minimum terms must be served before parole can be given, and suspension of sentence is allowed only for first offenses.

Second and subsequent offenses include out-of-state convictions relating to narcotic drugs or marijuana.

Wisconsin

To possess or be in control of marijuana is punishable by not more than one year in the county jail and a fine of up to $500 for a first offense. There is a provision, discretionary with the court, for probation without a verdict.

A subsequent offense is punishable by not more than two years in prison and a fine of up to $1,000.

The sale of marijuana is punishable by imprisonment for not more than five years and a fine of up to $5,000.

A subsequent offense is punishable by imprisonment for not more than ten years and a fine of up to $5,000.

The sale of marijuana or narcotic drugs to a person under twenty-one is punishable by imprisonment for not less than three nor more than twenty-five years, not less than twenty years nor more than life for a second offense, and life imprisonment for a third offense. Parole, probation, and suspension of the sentence is allowed in all cases, except for a second offense for sale to a minor.

Wyoming

The possession, control, receiving, buying, concealing, or compounding of any narcotic drug (including marijuana) is punishable by a jail term of not more than six months and a fine of up to $1,000 for a first offense, not more than five years in prison and a fine of up to $2,000 for a second offense, and not more than ten years and a fine of up to $2,000 for a third offense.

Selling, dispensing, or administering marijuana or any narcotic drug to a person twenty-one or over, or inducing a person over twenty-one to use marijuana or a narcotic drug is punishable by imprisonment for not more than ten years for a first offense, and not more than twenty-five years for a second offense.

Selling, dispensing, or administering marijuana or any narcotic drug to a person under twenty-one or inducing a person under twenty-one to use marijuana or any narcotic drug is punishable by not more than twenty years for a first offense, and not more than fifty years for a second offense.

Second and subsequent offenses include out-of-state felonies relating to narcotic drugs.

The following short list of books and articles includes a wide range of opinion on the subject of drugs. For further references, some of them have their own bibliographies.

Books

Advisory Committee on Drug Dependence. *Cannabis.* London: Her Majesty's Stationery Office, 1968.

American Medical Association. *Drug Dependence: A Guide for Physicians.* Chicago: American Medical Association, 1969.

Cohen, Sidney. *The Beyond Within: The LSD Story.* New York: Atheneum Publishers, 1964.

Coles, Robert. *The Grass Pipe.* Boston: Little, Brown & Co., 1969.

Huxley, Aldous. *The Doors of Perception.* New York: Harper & Row, Publishers, 1954.

Keniston, Kenneth. *The Uncommitted: Alienated Youth in American Society.* New York: Dell Publishing Co., Inc., 1967.

Klüver, Heinrich. *Mescal and Mechanisms of Hallucinations.* Chicago: University of Chicago Press, 1966.

Selected bibliography

Leary, Timothy. *The Politics of Ecstasy.* New York: G. P. Putnam's Sons, 1969.

Louria, Donald B. *The Drug Scene.* New York: McGraw-Hill Book Company, 1968.

Nowlis, Helen H. *Drugs on the College Campus.* New York: Doubleday & Company, Inc., Anchor Books, 1969.

Solomon, David, ed. *The Marihuana Papers.* Indianapolis: The Bobbs-Merrill Co., Inc., 1966.

Articles

Carey, James T. "Marihuana use among the New Bohemians." *Journal of Psychedelic Drugs* (Haight-Ashbury Medical Clinic) 2:1, 79–88 (1968).

Farnsworth, Dana L. "The drug problem among young people." *West Virginia Medical Journal* 63:433–437 (1967).

Farnsworth, Dana L. "Drugs—their use and abuse by college students." In *Psychiatry, Education, and the Young Adult.* Springfield, Ill.: Charles C. Thomas Publisher, 1966.

Frosch, W. A.; Robbins, E. S.; and Stern, M. "Untoward Reactions to Lysergic Acid Diethylamide (LSD) Resulting in Hospitalization." *New England Journal of Medicine* 273:1235–1239 (1965).

Ginsberg, Allen. "The Great Marijuana Hoax." *The Atlantic Monthly* 218:104–112 (November, 1966).

Grinspoon, Lester. "Marihuana." *Scientific American* 221:6, 19–25 (December, 1969).

Leary, Timothy. "Interview with Leary." *Playboy Magazine* 13:93 (September, 1966).

McGlothlin, W. H. "Hallucinogenic Drugs: A Perspective with special reference to Peyote and Cannabis." *Psychedelic Review* 6:16–57 (1965).

Smith, David E. "LSD and the Psychedelic Syndrome." *Clinical Toxicology* 2:1, 69–73 (1969).

Smith, David E. "The Characteristics of Dependence in High-Dose Methamphetamine Abuse." *International Journal of the Addictions* 4:3, 453–459 (1969).

Selected bibliography

Snyder, S. H.; Faillace, L.; Hollister, L. "2,5-Dimethoxy-4-methyl-amphetamine (STP): A New Hallucinogenic Drug." *Science* 158: 669–670 (1967).

Ungerleider, J. T.; Fisher, D. D.; and Fuller, M. "The Dangers of LSD." *Journal of the American Medical Association* 197:389–392 (1966).

Weil, A. T.; Zinberg, N. E.; and Nelsen, J. M. "Clinical and Psychological Effects of Marihuana in Man." *Science* 162:1234–1242 (1968).

Yolles, Stanley F. Statement on LSD, marijuana, and other dangerous drugs before the Senate Subcommittee on Juvenile Delinquency, 6 March, 1968.

| Index

Drugs and Youth

Quinn, Robert, 164

Reality, 47, 66
Reefers, 19
Relaxation feelings, 6, 132
Religious experiences, 67, 147
Research on drugs, 181–183
    on marijuana, 22, 26–27, 160–163
Resistance to drugs, 14–15
Roberts, Burton B., 172
Rockefeller, Nelson, 164

St. Clair, James D., 179, 181–182
Schizophrenia, 61–63
Search and seizure, 184–196
    consent searches, 189–191
    illegal seizures, 193–197
    violation of Fourth Amendment,
        184–185, 188
    without warrants, 187
Seconal, 12
Self-discovery, 146–147
Sellers and pushers, 5, 28
    penalties for, 165, 175
Sensitivity, effects of marijuana,
    47–48, 132–133
Sentences for drug use, 201–202
    suspension of, 207–209
Set, 28–29, 50–51
Sexual relationships, 33–34
"Shooting speed," 15
"Skin-popping," 79–80
Sleeping pills, 13, 16
"Smack" (heroin), 79
Smith, Weldon H., 88
"Snort" (heroin), 79, 80
Southeast Asia, drug source, 19, 79
Space perception, 33, 38, 133–134
Speed (methamphetamine hydro-
    chloride), 15, 73–74
State drug laws, 155–157
    list of, 208–247
Stimulants and sedatives, 13
STP (DOM), 72
Suburban drug addiction, 86, 88–
    94, 98, 109–119, 123–124,
    148–150
    heroin use, 125
    marijuana use, 88–89, 91–93, 98
    psychological response to drugs,
        127–131, 152

Suicide attempts, 63, 154–155, 173
Sulphonamide drugs, 75–76
Supernova experience, 58
Supreme Court decisions, 176–177,
    183, 184
Suspiciousness, 36–38
Synesthesia, 52, 69
Synthetic drugs, 3, 23, 76

Tauro, G. Joseph, 179, 181–183
"Tea" (marijuana), 19, 68
THC (tetrahydrocannabinols),
    22–23
Time perception, 31–32, 52–53,
    70, 133
Tolerance to drugs, 4, 14–15, 73

Uniform Narcotic Drug Act, 157,
    165
United Nations Commission on
    Narcotics, 7
United Nations International Nar-
    cotics Control Board, 79

Violence, not caused by marijuana,
    3, 8–9

Wall Street Journal, 22
Warrants, 184–196, 202
    challenging, 200, 202
    illegal, 196–198, 202
    searches without, 187
Warren, Earl, 176
Weber, Max, 98
"Weed" (marijuana), 19
Weight control drugs, 15, 73
Weil, Dr. Andrew, 27
White House Conference of Gov-
    ernors on Drug Abuse, 158,
    163–164
Wilde, Oscar, 35
Withdrawal symptoms, 15, 84–85
Wood, Dr. Alexander, 80
Woodstock rock festival, 168
Wyzanski, Charles J., 173–174

Yolles, Dr. Stanley, 88n
Youth culture, 86, 98–99, 119–
    120, 147
    See also Adolescence